The enterprise as story

The role of narrative in enterprise-architecture

Tom Graves

Tetradian Consulting

Published by
Tetradian Books
Unit 215, Communications House
9 St Johns Street, Colchester, Essex CO2 7NN
England

http://www.tetradianbooks.com

First published February 2012
ISBN 978-1-906681-34-0 (paperback)
ISBN 978-1-906681-35-7 (e-book)

Contents

Acknowledgements

Amongst others, the following people kindly provided comments and feedback on themes in the various drafts of this book: Peter Bakker (NL), Stuart Boardman (NL), Shawn Callahan (AU), Pat Ferdinandi (US), Bas van Gils (NL), Nigel Green (GB), Paul Hobcraft (CH), Anders Jensen (AU), Gerold Kathan (AT), Cynthia Kurtz (US), Michael Margolis (US), James McGovern (US), Liz Poraj-Wilczynska (GB), Kevin Smith (GB), Michael Smith (MX), David Tebbutt (GB), David Topping (GB), Peter Tseglakof (AU)

Please note that, to preserve commercial and personal confidentiality, the stories and examples in this book will usually have been adapted, combined and in part fictionalised from experiences in a variety of contexts, and do not and are not intended to represent any specific individual or organisation.

Registered trademarks such as Zachman, TOGAF, FEAF, ITIL, Business Model Canvas etc are acknowledged as the intellectual property of the respective owners.

INTRODUCTION

The enterprise as story

"What's the story?" – would that be an unusual phrase to start a business-book? Perhaps so, but it does seems appropriate here...

Once upon a time, we might say, I started out on a metaphorical journey to explore the role of story in the enterprise, and especially story in relation to enterprise-architectures. It's been a strange journey, at times a very fraught one, yet also a worthwhile one. And one that does seem worth sharing with others. Hence, here, with you. A story about the enterprise *as* story.

Who is this for?

As with the other books in this series, I'll assume that you're working as an enterprise-architect, business-architect, strategist, process-designer or some such. That's the 'intended audience', if you like.

But it actually doesn't matter: unlike some of my more technical books, this one really *is* relevant for just about everyone who works in organisations. Story is for everyone: that's the whole point of what you'll find here.

What's in this book?

I'll say up front that this is a bit different from the usual approach I've used in other books. There is, of course, a good reason why.

As with most current conventional approaches to enterprise-architectures, most of my work to date has focussed on structure. Often a much broader view of structure than others might hold, perhaps – such as 'everything as a service', or the structures of relationships and intent – but structure nonetheless.

Yet that's only one side of the enterprise-architecture story. Literally so – because just as structure is everywhere and every-thing in enterprise-architecture, so is story. Story is *everywhere*. That's what makes it important. That's also, at times, what makes it hard.

1

The usual way to describe structure is through structure: hence the formal-style structure with most of my previous books, partitioned into themes and topics and the like, each with their own section about how to apply it in practice. In the same way, it seems the best approach to describe story is via story: hence a sort-of-story about story in enterprise-architecture, and about the stories, and the many layers and types and forms of story, that interweave with each other to make up the enterprise *as* story.

There *is* a structure here, of course, though we might describe it as somewhat post-modern in style: kind of structure-beyond-structure. Themes and phrases will recur and repeat at times – as you may have noticed already – yet that too *is* intentional, the repetition providing not just re-emphasis but also often another view into the same overall 'holograph' that is the enterprise.

In the same way, the story may often seem fragmentary at times, things described only in part, as if seen from a distance – because that's exactly how we see a whole at each moment, with sense and structure of that whole emerging only over time, and only in its own way, beyond our direct command and control. (That's part of why this has been the most difficult book so far for me to write – but also one of the most rewarding.)

So it's a story about story, in a context where most people don't seem much to notice the stories, and for the most part don't seem to acknowledge their importance either. The story so far, perhaps?

Yet every book in this series is about practice, about *usefulness*, about ideas that we can put to immediate use in the everyday work of enterprise-architecture. So in keeping with the other books, there's one concession that I'll make here to the need for structure: I'll end each chapter with a brief summary-section, labelled 'Application', summarising key points from the preceding text, with suggestions about how to apply those ideas in your own real-world context. There's also a list of references and resources in an Appendix at the end of the book.

Anyway, enough for now: on to the story.

01: EVERYDAY ENTERPRISE-ARCHITECTURE

What's the story? It's another day here in everyday enterprise-architecture: all the usual tasks, the usual models, the usual analysis-work and review-meetings and all the rest. A lot of work still, to link everything together across that whole range of structures that we work with: data-structures, organisational-structures, process-structures, infrastructures, whatever.

All satisfying in its own way, of course. If nothing else, there's a great professional challenge for our team in all of this, in creating clarity, consistency, sense. And of real value to the business: we can prove that now, too.

And yet… there's something… odd… not quite right? Like there's something *missing*? A blind-spot, maybe; something huge, even; yet can't see what it might be *because* it isn't there? That kind of feeling. Disconcerting. Worrying. Or worse.

It's the same sort of feeling that was around when we first started our work on enterprise-architecture. Back then, everything was centred only around IT, an *IT-centric* view of the organisation, as if IT was the only thing that mattered in the whole enterprise; most of what they'd called 'business-architecture' would be more accurately described as 'anything not-IT that might affect IT'. Useless, really; or misleading, at any rate. But things *have* changed over the past few years: there's a lot more awareness of business-strategy, of business *as* business. The claim to be *enterprise-*architecture now looks a lot more credible these days: much more of a meeting of minds with the business-folk.

Yet still there are those nagging doubts… We see it, perhaps, in that so often there's so much of a *struggle* to get things going, to get people onside. It's not a problem of scope any more: we really do have much more of an enterprise-wide scope. It seems more that although our models and so on make perfect sense to us, they don't seem to make sense to anyone else. They're not *connecting*, somehow. But why not? That doesn't make sense either…

That nagging uncertainty takes me back to an odd incident at the launch of a new version of a well-known enterprise-architecture

3

framework. In the midst of all the hoo-ha and self-celebration, one of their team pulls me aside. "You know what's missing in all of this?" he says, in a whisper, as if afraid to be overheard. "There's no place in it anywhere for *people*."

He's right: there isn't. People are mentioned occasionally almost in passing, perhaps as inputs to processes, but nowhere *as* people in their own right. Odd... Yet what does that absence imply for the architecture – or for the enterprise that uses that architecture?

Another memory comes up. This time I'm on a train, reading Matthew Frederick's *101 Things I Learned in Architecture School*. It's about building-architecture, not enterprise-architecture, yet it's clear that many of the same principles do apply to both. The book is laid out in simple two-page spreads, sketch-drawing on one side, a brief pithy summary on the other. As I turn the page, the text all but leaps out at me:

> **Two points of view on architecture**:
>
> *Architecture is an exercise in **truth**. A proper building is responsible to universal knowledge and is wholly honest in the expression of its functions and materials.*
>
> *Architecture is an exercise in **narrative**. Architecture is a vehicle for the telling of stories, a canvas for relaying societal myths, a stage for the theater of everyday life.*

Truth and narrative; the structure and the story. All of those conventional EA-frameworks focus on the certainties of structure – "it's all about IT processes and data", as one somewhat-myopic colleague used to insist – leaving no place within them for story *as* story. Yet if there's no story, there's no place for people – which is *why* there's no place in it for people.

Which is why, in that kind of purported 'enterprise'-architecture, there's actually no place in it for *enterprise*. The enterprise *is* people: enterprise is what people *do*. But if the architecture has no place for people, then those people can't be enterpris*ing* within it: and we then wonder why we have enterprises that fail...

And no wonder we have a problem with the architecture, too: in an all too literal sense, if we only work on structure, we'd only be delivering one half of the actual architecture. Oops...

But if enterprise-architecture is missing its story, what *is* that story? How do we find it? And how do we embed it or link it into the architectures that we already have?

What's the story? Clearly, something that needs to be explored...

Application

- Is that true for you? – that the story of enterprise architecture seems to be missing its story?
- What, to you, is 'story'? Where – if at all – does it apply in enterprise-architecture?
- Which types of stories are included at present in the architecture? How are they used? What do they add, and how, and why?
- What are the missing stories? – the types of stories that we need, but aren't there, or aren't visible? And if the stories are missing, what impact does that absence have on your enterprise-architecture, and on the enterprise as a whole?

INTERLUDE

Earlier this week I'd spent a long session with two colleagues, talking about how our respective business-models have had to adapt over the years, to re-align with changing needs and changing perceptions in the marketplace. Without much noticing that we're doing so, we describe each change with a story, about letting go of the legacy of the past, and of what we learn from and through the change. A biography of a business, told in stories. And stories within stories, as anchor for meaning, and as compass: by changing the story, we change the direction.

So it's the weekend now, a different café, a different conversation. A friend's 50th-birthday party: he's proudly wearing a badge that says "21 Today! (29th anniversary)" – a small icon that says so much about our culture's attitudes to age. I'm seated opposite his late-teenage daughter, and we strike up a conversation about what she's doing, her classes at college, her photography, her hopes and fears for the future. It doesn't take long until the stories start to flow – some of them taking me back too many decades, to when I faced much the same fraught times and temperaments. Stories as connection; stories as challenge...

The meal over, we continue the conversation outside. Out there in the street, there's a young man of about her age, busking with a full drum-kit and backing-track. He's drawn quite a crowd there, though many of them more interested in the antics of the old man who's dancing quietly to the music, over on the far side. He's well into his eighties, at a guess, and a lot of people are laughing at him: I'm not, because it's clear he's not 'showing off', or knowingly making a fool of himself in public, he knows exactly what he's doing, with the music, and the dance. He knows he's being mocked, but he doesn't care: he's only interested in the music, and what it means to him. And he dances on, with care, precision, locked exactly to the beat, and with much more energy and stamina than one might expect from someone of that age. A drummer himself, I'd guess, not so many years ago.

I'd been searching for a story to show her how we can't depend on inspiration alone, that it comes and goes whether we like it or not, and hence how and why we need all those 'boring' predictable patterns to fall back on, to keep us going and to continue to do *something* useful until the inspiration does return. Which it always does – *if* we allow it to do so, and if we don't try to control how and when it does. And yet here's the perfect story, right here in the street, in the old man's dance. As the music rolls on, most of the time he's right there, 'in the groove'. From time to time, though, he loses the connection: for a moment, the inspiration that drives the dance is gone. Yet he doesn't try to control it, to force the dance; and neither does he just give up and stop. Instead, he falls back to a pattern, swaying gently from side to side, still listening closely with his whole body to the beat, keeping a space open for the inspiration to return. Which it does: suddenly he's back in the groove again, dancing with 'the flow' as much as with the dance itself. A real inspiration: and, clearly, a lot of stories behind the surface story.

Application

- Looking at your own organisation – or your own business-life – in what ways has 'the story' changed over the years? At each stage, what was let go, what was learned? What was lost? What was more a liberation? What's the story there?

- Looking back, what stories do you tell yourself, and others, about those times – both of the periods of continuity, when things seemed stable for a while, and of the transitions, those times of uncertainty that were somehow 'between stories'?

- What cultural clues do you see from the small stories, such as in that 'not-21st-birthday' badge? What can you learn from similar 'small stories' within your own organisation?

- In what ways do stories create a connection between you and others? How do they connect across time, across generations? In what ways could such stories help to create connection and shared-learning across your own organisation?

- What are the stories that create energy, stamina, drive – even in the face of mockery and other opposition? Where would such stories have most impact in your own enterprise?

- Where do you find stories and parables to illustrate particular points in your architecture? How do you create the space to allow yourself to notice suitable stories serendipitously, from what's happening around you in the moment?

02: WHAT'S THE STORY?

Staring at the whiteboard, for hours on end, trying to find *any* pattern in that blizzard of sticky-notes and scrawls. One question keeps coming back, time after time: *What's the story?*

Stuck. We all know *that* feeling...

Step back a bit: what's the story behind the story? Well, that part's straightforward, I guess. I'd been invited to do a presentation at a conference on enterprise-architecture. I knew the audience would be broader than just the stereotypic 'finance, banking, insurance, tax' of so much mainstream EA, so it would give me a chance to try something new: the role of story in enterprise-architecture. I'd already explored various aspects of this in various posts on my weblog, so it shouldn't be difficult. And yet it is: I'm stuck, going round and round, on just one question: What's the story? What's the theme that will hold it all together? I can find enough of a story-line with which to do the presentation – but not story *itself*. There's something strange here that I can't pin down...

Structure and story; the structure is already there throughout our enterprise-architectures, but the story isn't. Yet looking across the EA discipline as a whole, everywhere there's the same kind of imbalance as that between structure and story:

- *content versus context* – just about everything we see describes content, often seemingly divorced from any context...
- *'control' versus trust* – a lot of emphasis on would-be 'control', not much on trust...
- *organisation versus enterprise* - many people seem to think that the organisation *is* the enterprise...
- *certainty versus uncertainty* – it's almost like uncertainty isn't allowed – yet the real world *is* uncertain...
- *sameness versus difference* - again, the same drive to try to make everything the same, certain, predictable – which the real world isn't...
- *rules versus principles* – huge emphasis on 'the letter of the law', yet not much about the *intent* in 'the spirit of the law'...
- *machines versus people* – not much room for people *as* people, pretty much anywhere...

The balance between structure and story – or lack of it – seems similarly skewed, yet also seemingly linked to everything else. So perhaps if we focus on story, we might also help bring those other themes back into better balance too.

So what *is* story? And where *does* it occur within our enterprise-architectures?

The short answer is: *everywhere.*

Every use-case is a story – a story of what we want to happen.

Every scenario is a story of what *might* happen.

Every customer-journey is a story-in-progress; likewise every transaction, even right down at the level of two computer-systems talking to each other; a transaction-protocol is a proto-story.

In marketing, the whole point of a brand is that it tells a story – a story of hope, desire, intent, of use and usefulness, of longing and belonging.

Every learning is a change of story; every change-project likewise aims to change a story.

A supply-chain is a story; a strategy is a story; even the enterprise itself is a story.

And so on, and so on, and so on: story is so *much* 'everywhere' that it's sometimes hard to see...

So *why* story? What's so important about story? Why does it matter?

This time the answer's not quite so short, but in essence it's the distinction between *content* and *context* – the 'things' of the world, versus the *usefulness* of those things. The physical world is made of atoms, but the human world is made of stories. Within a business, within its architecture, we might have all the 'things' we need to make everything work; but without the stories, there's no meaning, no purpose, no reason or drive to *do* anything with those things – and hence no *enterprise*. Which also means no business. Hence why, yes, this *matters*...

More subtle, perhaps, is a trap pointed out many centuries ago by Lao Tsu, in the *Tao Te Ching*:

> "Profit comes from what is there;
> usefulness from what is not there".

If we're developing an architecture for a commercial business, there'll no doubt be a lot of focus on profit – sometimes almost to the exclusion of everything else. Yet whilst the profit may arise from 'what is there' – from "the ten thousand things", to use Lao Tsu's phrase – the 'usefulness', the way we *create* that profit, comes from 'what is not there', the connections *between* things, the stories. So if we can't see the stories – because they're seemingly 'not there' – we'd then have no way to reach that profit. Hence, again, this *matters*.

Finally, another quote that caught my eye the other day, this time from Christina Baldwin:

> "Words are how we think; stories are how we link"

Words are easy; it's finding the story that's hard. And the same is true in our architectures, the age-old distinction between 'boxes and lines'. The boxes in all those myriad diagrams represent the 'things', whilst the lines represent the connections *between* things. And yet so many of those diagrams are static – literally so, since they claim to describe some past or current or future state. What we rarely see are the dynamics, the *stories* that traverse those lines connecting everything together. So to make the architecture work – to bring it to life – we need to balance the structure with the stories.

Finding the stories might well be a way to get unstuck, too...

Application

- Where do you get stuck – in particular, stuck in terms of ideas and issues at work? What's the story behind that sense of 'stuckness'?
- What are the stories that you see in your architecture, your organisation, your enterprise? What is it that *makes* it a story?
- "Profit comes from what is there; usefulness from what is not there" – What does this suggest about your own organisation and its architecture? Is the focus only on 'what is there', or does it also include 'what is not there'?
- And by what means can you see 'what is not there'? Or explain it, or even describe it, in your architecture? How can you describe what's missing from 'what is not there'?
- 'Boxes and lines': you'll see plenty of those in your architecture diagrams. But what are the stories that link those 'boxes' together? And how *do* these stories traverse those metaphoric lines?

10

INTERLUDE

It's *all* about story. All of it.

Enterprise-architecture is all about story. The enterprise itself is a story; but the practice of enterprise-architecture is all about stories too. Let me tell you a story...

There once was this half-crazed guy who used to go on about an even crazier idea that there might be a bit more to enterprise-architecture than just, well, IT-boxes and suchlike. That there was a bit more to the story than that.

It starts, like most good stories, a long time ago. Turns out that whilst he'd arrived at EA via the usual IT-journey, from years of assembly-language through to database-design through to data-architecture and information and the rest, that wasn't where he really came from. (I don't think he's the long-lost Prince of Multigravia, though - it's not that kind of story. Sorry.)

He'd actually started out in graphic design, getting sidetracked into software and stuff to try to get typesetting-systems to work better. And he hadn't forgotten the designer's way of thinking about things (which these days goes by the fancy term of 'design-thinking', but it wasn't called anything much back then). It was always about thinking about the big-picture at the same time as looking at the small-picture, and keeping the tension in balance whilst going in deeper and smaller and smaller and smaller, whilst still keeping the big-picture and the bigger-picture and the really-really-big-picture all in view at the same time. Kinda crazy-making, but that's designers for you, of course.

And then something happened. (Yep, that's a phrase that comes a lot in stories.) He was working on enterprise-architecture by then, the usual tedium of tracking down all those tiddy little Access databases and spreadsheets that were being used way outside of their scope or capability. Oh joys. But one area he was asked to look at in this was quality-management. Which brought up a simple yet surprisingly scary question: what *is* quality, anyway?

Quality can be very tricky indeed: not a popular topic with many business-folks. So unpopular in this case that the quality-manager had committed suicide. (That part isn't a story, sadly...) So how are they going to manage quality? We know how to do it, they said – we can do it all with software! Buy an off-the-shelf package from one of the big vendors, plug it in, roll it out to the whole workforce – there, problem solved! Easy! It's a few million bucks and ongoing but so what, it's just 'fit and forget', isn't it...?

Uh. No. Even our half-crazed anti-hero could see that it wouldn't work. The problem was that lots of people wanted to believe that it would. Lots of serious business people with serious career-ambitions, and with serious access to lots of other people's money. (Are these the villains of the story? Perhaps – but we'd better not say so in public if we want to keep our jobs?) A tricky enterprise-architecture problem, that one... But with a lot of hunting around, amongst the few mostly hidden backroom-boys still holding out the flag for the not-quite-lost quality-cause, we found an in-house team who'd developed a quality-system that really did work. All done on little pieces of paper. No IT at all.

Sure, they were moving some parts onto software, but that was just a simple customisation of a 'knowledge-management' system for which we already had a site-wide licence, and which almost no-one else seemed to be using anyway. Straight away a serious saving of several million dollars. But the main point was that it worked. *And it was all about stories.* Making sense, through stories.

Getting people to work together, to get the work together and make it work better.

Finding the best way to do the work, in whatever combination of people, machines and IT would be the best fit to that particular context.

Exploring, enquiring, endless seeking, ceaselessly improving. A commitment to quality; an enterprise in itself.

All through stories.

Which is itself a story.

So where are all of those stories in our usual narratives about enterprise-architecture? Uh... still nowhere to be seen? Oops...

Perhaps this all too usual story of enterprise-architecture needs a different ending...?

Application

- What are *your* architecture stories? When you're faced with a horror-story such as that of the quality-manager above, where would you find the counter-story to make things right?

- Do you work with people who assume that every business-problem can be solved with some kind of pre-packaged IT-system? – and that that option must by definition be the best choice, solely *because* it's IT-based, and therefore 'known' and 'certain'?

- If so, how do you get your colleagues to explore the wider story, and perhaps seek for simpler, more maintainable solutions? How do you engage them in a story that might revolve around *people*, rather than solely around IT?

03: NARRATIVE AND STORY

So what *is* story, anyway? What is it that makes story different from anything else? And when we're describing the structures of an architecture, isn't that a story too?

Well, sort-of, I guess... Structure itself is just structure: there's no story there, as such. But we tell stories *about* structure, *around* structure; structure as backdrop to story, the stage upon which stories are set. Structure is structure: it doesn't have much *meaning* until there's a story. Architecture is both structure *and* story, is both truth *and* narrative; the one doesn't make much sense without the other.

Yet if we look at most of the EA tools that we have, and the EA methods that we have, they're all about structure. They're very good on structure – no doubt about that. Unfortunately, though, they're *not* good on narrative, or story. There are a few notable exceptions, but for the others...? – well, apart from a few brief excursions into use-cases and the like, they're not much use on narrative... not so much 'no-story' as a negation of story itself.

Oh.

Which is a much more serious problem than it looks, because in practice, most of our enterprise-architecture work is actually about stories. Stories upon stories: lots of them.

Again, look around: story is *everywhere* – hard to see only because it *is* so much 'everywhere'. Every strategy tells a story – a story of a different future. Every merger or demerger or restructure or reorganisation or re-whatever is a story, a change of story. On the smaller scale, a business-scenario is a story. A use-case is a story. From as-is to to-be is a story. A typical application-consolidation effort is a story too, about how to clean up the tangle of this-doesn't-go-with-that, and change it to a new story of and-they-all-lived-happily-ever-after (until the next consolidation, anyway). It's all stories.

Every requirement implies a story. The work of an Agile team is all about co-creating a shared story. And getting people to work together is a story in itself, and one that in itself is so often made up of people sharing their different perspectives on what should end up as a shared story – perhaps across the whole enterprise.

Enterprise-architecture, in this sense, is all about supporting those stories. Every model tells a story, a record of decisions, options, choices. We can use each model to elicit further stories: people disagree with the choice, perhaps give us their story of why the choice needs to change; perhaps they agree, and the story helps to reaffirm and reinforce that choice, that story.

Yet at the moment, almost none of that is in the models. Or, for that matter, the methods. We're somehow supposed to know it's all about story – but somehow pretend it's all about the IT instead. Odd…

And when we stop to think about it, enterprise-architects don't actually *do* much other than tell stories, or get others to tell stories. We don't do much development-work, perhaps not any: that's the solution-architects' job, and they'll often get annoyed if we tread too much on their turf, their story. We don't have much authority – especially beyond the borders of our own organisation. In most cases all we *can* do is influence, cajole, guide. And the way we do that is by creating a story.

It's all about stories.

And though I hadn't noticed it until now, that lack of support for the story is what's been so frustrating for me about so many of the existing toolsets, too: it's not that their near-exclusive focus on structure is somehow 'wrong' or whatever, but it's because it stifles the story. Some of the toolsets are so constrained and so clunky that it's like being a captive in kindergarten again, where the only permissible poems must be modelled on 'Mary Had A Little Lamb'. The obsessive IT-centrism in so much architecture is like the self-centred bar-room bore, who insists that they have to be the hero of everyone's else story. (The business-centrism of so many business-architecture tools is no better, by the way.) And a half-assed, half-complete story is no story at all. No fun for anyone else, anyway.

As enterprise-architects, we need to engage people in change, in a vision of something that works better than they have at present. And that's why we need toolsets and methods that can cover the whole scope, the whole story of the enterprise, and support us in our storytelling of that story – because we need them to engage themselves in that broader story.

Enterprise-architecture: it's all about stories. So it might help to remember that fact – by telling a story or two, perhaps?

Yet how *do* we tell an architecture-story? And story and narrative: aren't they the same? Again, the answer's 'sort-of': they're both about sequence of action in context, "something happened, and then something else happened, and then something else...". With narrative, that's just about all we get; but a story is, well, a *story*.

Narrative is important – don't get me wrong about that. We use narrative all the time in architectures. For example, consider a UML (Unified Modelling Language) Sequence Diagram or State Transition Diagram – all the *behaviour-diagrams*, as contrasted with UML's structure-diagrams. Each of those is a visual description of 'something should happen, and then something else should happen', with branches in the sequence to show what should happen in this case, or that case, or the other case. Something happens; and then something else happens. That's narrative.

There are variants of that kind of narrative, of course. There's a *protocol*, a kind of pre-planned narrative between two entities, describing who should do what and when, and in response to what and when – again, a sequence of action in context, but this time of *shared*-action in context. And the overall 'conversation' can involve more than two entities, of course: consider a supply-chain sequence from supplier's-supplier to customer's-customer, or the links between swimlanes in a BPMN (Business Process Modeling Notation) process-diagram. Yet it's still just a narrative: something happens, and then something else happens.

The problem with narrative alone is that it's, well, *boring*... It's like sitting in on someone else's slideshow of "What we saw on our holidays": sure, something happened, and then something else happened, all nicely illustrated with pretty pictures and the like – but so what? Where's the *story*?

So much of our current architectures are like that slideshow: lots of narrative, lots of structure in the background, lots of pretty diagrams, but where's the story? There's nothing to *engage* people's attention, to answer the inevitable questions:

- what does it mean?
- what's the point?
- where do *I* fit in this story?
- what's in it for me?

That's the real difference between 'mere narrative', and story. Narrative tells us the what and how and when and who and sometimes where; and, when well-done, does it well. But story adds that crucial all-too-often-absent element of *why* – the *purpose*, the *meaning* behind the narrative.

Story gives us the reason why that sequence of action in context should happen in the first place. Story shows us what we can learn from what happened. Narrative alone is often too abstract to make sense; story makes it *real*, tangible, concrete – despite being just as imaginary as the narrative itself.

That's why *story*, rather than solely the narrative. That's why story *matters* in our architecture, why structure alone is not enough – because without the story that accompanies that description of the structure, there's no meaning, no point.

With the story, there *is* a point. A stakeholder asks us "What's in it for me?": a story explains exactly what's in it for them, places them *in* the story, makes it *their* story too. Many architects I speak with complain about how difficult it is to 'sell' their architecture to the stakeholders: yet if we build it around story, it sells itself. A lot simpler than hard-sell...

One key difference here between narrative and story is 'the unexpected': "we were doing this, and doing that, and then doing this as well, *and then something unexpected happened*". It engages the people's attention; it introduces the possibility, of, well, *possibility*, really. Scary, yet hopeful, all at the same time.

For me, working on this book, the main 'the unexpected' in the story so far isn't about what's happened, but much more about what *hasn't* happened. By this stage I would expect to be working to an outline that I'd planned out, step by step, weeks or even months ago. But that just hasn't happened. I can't find the structure; can't find the story. All I have at present is a huge pile of notes, a great big hole of uncertainty that's loosely labelled 'Magic Happens Here' – so often the case in architecture-development! – and a single tag-line to which I keep coming back, and coming back, and coming back: *What's the story?*

The story's in there somewhere: I'm certain of that. Yet at present that's just about the only thing I *am* certain about: for everything else, right now, I'm stuck with having to 'wing it' until more of the clarity comes through. Uncomfortable. Very.

And yet that's not at all unusual at this stage of most architecture-work. So often I've sat with colleagues, staring at wall-fulls of diagrams and charts and summaries and other information, waiting for some kind of sense to settle out of the chaos in front of us. Sometimes it just takes its own time: and the more we push it, the further away it seems to get.

So in a sense, right now the story here is that there isn't a story. Except that there *is* a story. Somewhere. Just have to wait it out, I guess. Or rather, keep going, keep it moving, working on some part of structure that might help the story to coalesce. Structure and story intertwine: working on story helps us find the right structure, and working on structure helps us find the right story.

Which suggests that the best thing to work on for now would be the structure of story itself. Play with that for a while, and see what comes out of that.

Application

- What examples of narrative – sequences of action in context – do you see in your architectures?
- Where's the story? Much of architecture will focus on What and How, but where's the Why that makes it a *story*, something that *engages*? Where's the uncertainty that engages the interest?
- How much of your architecture-development consists of 'winging it', finding ways to cope with the unexpected, before you can get back the relative safety of structure, of the known? What's the story there?
- When you get stuck – especially at the big-picture level, as here – what do you do to get unstuck? What structure, what process, what habits, what tactics, do you turn to, in order to get the ball rolling again?

04: THE STRUCTURE OF STORY

What *is* a story? What's the *structure* of story?

Perhaps the best people we could turn to for help at this point would be the professional storytellers. For example, how does Hollywood structure a story? What do *they* think story is?

In a sense, they have the opposite problem to ours: our visible end-product is structure, and we need to support it with story; whereas their end-product is story, and they need to support it with structure. Overall, though, it *is* the same kind of problem: how to balance structure and story. The Goldilocks Challenge, we might say: not too much of either one or the other, but just the right amount of each.

And writing for the stage or screen – whether the big screen, the small screen, or the tiny handheld one – is a big business. *Very* big. Hence no surprise there's a *lot* of study on story and structure, and how to make them work together. The real challenge is to find the parts of structure that work well with *our* kind of story – the story of the enterprise and its architectures.

Some parts of story-structure – such as character-arc, for example – either don't fit with what we need, or at first may not seem to make much sense in our context. Yet there's a lot that does align very well with our needs in architecture: viewpoint, for example; or genre and mood, serial versus series, establishing the story, pacing, setup and payoff, possibility and probability, the real importance of the unexpected for surprise or delight, the problem of plot-holes – it's all there, ready for us to use in the architecture-story too. We just need to know how to adapt it, apply it...

One place we could start is with the screenplay, which, in a sense, is the architecture for the on-screen story. We could note, for example, just how efficient – or more, how *effective* – a screenplay has to be: it's no different from any other architecture in that respect. It takes a lot of skill, and a lot of work, to trim the five-hundred-plus pages of a Harry Potter novel all the way down to a sparse hundred pages of dialogue and direction.

Most standard screenplays are structured such that each page represents just one minute of screen-time: and everything has to be there on that single page. Every page has to carry the *essence* of the story, at every moment, without ever losing connection with that core; and every page, every line, every phrase, has to carry the story forward, with not a single word to waste. Taut; elegant; spare: those are some of the words we might use to describe a great screenplay.

And yet that screenplay is just the start of the production story. Look at those end-credits again: every film or show is a huge collaborative effort, involving tens, hundreds, maybe thousands of people, all with different skills to bear. Each will view the story and screenplay in their different way; each will bring their own insights to the story. Which means they'll usually want to change the story, too, to make things easier or more interesting for their own department. Hence the role of the architects – the director and, perhaps even more, the producer – to invite and encourage all these different views, and yet still hold true at all times to the essence of the story. That's not easy: we've all seen films that fall apart into a muddled mess somewhere. Yet the real masters make it seem so easy, so seamless, that we don't notice it at all: an interesting and important criterion for success...

Anyway, let's get back to the structure of story, in terms of the architecture of the enterprise.

If we ask the storytellers what to do here, they'd probably point us to the 'Hero's Journey' story-structure. This structure is so often used that some people claim that it's the *only* possible story – which I somewhat doubt, but it's certainly true that parts of it have become Hollywood clichés. For example, if you've ever wondered why there's an abrupt change around halfway through a story, or why there's some kind of death or bleak ending at the three-quarter point, or why the hero or some other key character seems to die (but usually recovers) just before the end, yes, it's because they're using the Hero's Journey pattern.

Which, at first glance, suggests we need to know that pattern if we're going to have any chance to understand the story side of enterprise-architecture.

So, start with a reminder of that point that screenplays are written in a format where one page equates to one minute of story-time. We could use page-counts to indicate how far through the story each key point in that pattern would occur; but since a typical Hollywood story runs for around a hundred minutes, we'll make it simpler and use percentages instead:

- *Before the start*: "someone toils long into the night", often for many years.

This is the 'backstory' for the story, which we'd usually find out through small dribs-and-drabs of information or 'exposition' as the story moves along. For a business or other enterprise, there's usually a lot of backstory: as someone put it, "it takes many years' hard work to become an overnight success…".

- *During 1-5%*: start with a strong opening image, to establish the 'ordinary world' for our lead character.

For most enterprise-architecture, this is would be that everyday world of structures and models, all centred around IT and the like. And yet there'd also be those niggling doubts and subtle hints that suggest something is seriously wrong – which leads us to:

- *At around 5%*: a trigger-event, an 'inciting incident' or 'call to adventure'.

Sometimes this might be 'something bad happens', sometimes something unexpectedly good, but either way it's a wake-up call of some kind. In business, this might just be the 'initiating event' for a business-process; for me here, the inciting-incident was two-fold, that comment about "there's no nowhere for people", and the note about 'architecture as narrative'.

- *During 5-10%*: outline the nature of the 'special-world'.

One of the key points here is that the inciting-incident shows us a new possibility of some kind – referred to in the Hero's Journey pattern as the 'special world'. We then have an apparent choice, either to go into that special-world, or stay where we are. If we stay where we are, of course, there'll be no story – or, in sales terms, there'll be no sale.

- *At around 10%*: setup is complete, and initial opposition identified or implied…

For this example of enterprise-architecture, we've established that story is everywhere in the enterprise, so story is clearly important – yet just about everyone else is thinking only in terms of structure. There's certainly a conflict there – and conflict, we're told, is the core to any good story.

- *During 10-25%*: …the hero refuses the call to adventure.

And I'll admit that's probably what I'm doing right now: still trying to explain story in terms of structure, rather than 'story *as* story'… In the story-pattern, this is a stage that can go on for quite a while, with increasing pressures to move into the special-world, yet still persistent evasions of the call. (Salesfolk would recognise this stage as 'objections to the offer'.) But all that dithering and procrastination can't go on forever, because:

- *At around 25%*: point of no-return, an irreversible commitment – also known as 'crossing the first threshold'.

It's a decision-point – sometimes forced on the hero, sometimes a deliberate choice, but the key point is that now there's no turning back: we're in the special-world. Another key facet is that this isn't about analysis any more: like all real decisions at the moment of action, it's an *emotional* choice, not a 'rational' one. (Skilled sales-folk know that this is the moment to *stop* talking, and allow space for the choice to take place.)

- *During 25-45%*: 'fun and games' with tests, allies and enemies.

It's often incidents in this section that will end up in the trailer for the film. For a conventional story, it's here that we would establish 'the B-story', a secondary thread cutting across the theme – such as the standard-issue 'love-interest' in classic Hollywood action-movies. (Sales-folk might recognise this as the initial follow-up to the sale, showing extra options and possibilities that anchor the purchaser's satisfaction at their choice.)

Another common theme here, which usually won't become clear until later, is that during this stage we either 'go for the wrong goal', or a goal that is narrower in scope than that which is needed to resolve the key theme of the story. That's something I still need to identify for *this* context, on story in enterprise-architecture…

- *During 45-50%*: approach to the inmost cave.

What happens in that previous 'fun and games' is what we might describe as exploration of the *rational* outcomes of that decision to enter the special-world. At some key point we also start to hit up against the *emotional* side as well – and it's the emotion that drives the whole story. (Sales-folk would recognise this as another key signal to stop talking, and *listen* for a change in direction.)

- *At around 50%*: abrupt stop at midpoint – 'cross the second threshold', endure the ordeal and take the reward

There's an important emotional challenge at this point, usually where the protagonist must face huge inner doubts, and often either gains a new but more challenging ally, or is forced to go on alone without a key ally. (Sales-folk would know this as the first stage of 'buyer's remorse', where the prospect hits up against the emotional downside of the purchase, and wants to back out. It's essential to acknowledge that this *is* a challenge that the buyer must face alone: any help from the sales-person at this point will only make things worse, and possibly cost the sale.)

- *During 50-75%*: 'pursuit on the road' – renewed challenges, the antagonists close in

The 'fun and games' of the previous stage return, but this time with renewed intensity, and often with a change of allies, hence a new set of interpersonal dynamics. (Sales-folk might recognise this as the point where they hand over to another colleague to answer detailed technical questions, for example – and they too have to trust that the technical guy won't screw up the sale.)

Importantly, this section continues to 'go for the wrong goal' – still tackling only a subset of the real issues that drive the initial 'call to adventure'. (A first-hand example for many enterprise-architects is the way in which the over-emphasis on IT had masked the fact that even the IT-issues can only be resolved by becoming more aware of impacts across the whole shared-enterprise.)

- *At around 75%*: the 'all is lost' point, followed by the 'Dark Night Of The Soul'; then reversal, to 'cross the third threshold'

Often this takes the form of a 'double-whammy': an intensely personal and painful realisation that this path just isn't going to work – often accompanied by the loss of the most important ally – followed by a dawn of understanding that this wasn't the right path in the first place. There's a brief period of mourning, and then set off once more in a new direction. (Sales-folk would know this as the inverse version of 'buyer's remorse', where the buyer suddenly realises that what they've chosen and committed to will not actually do the task they need. This is the moment at which carefully-placed options for upselling become possible.)

- *During 75-85%*: increasing intensity and renewed pursuit in the push towards the new goal

This is another version of 'fun and games', except that now there's much more clarity about what the goal really is – and also the challenges to face in getting there.

- *During 85-90%*: a setback highlights the final challenge, and a rethink of the plan

The goal is clear, but the tactics to get there are not: this is the point about the often quite lengthy challenge-and-setback here. (Sales-folk would know this as the moment to re-frame the story, particularly if there's a need to support an upsell.)

- *During 90-95%*: climax – often as 'death and resurrection' – followed by final resolution

After a final struggle – often primarily personal and emotional – the goal is at last achieved, and the protagonist 'reborn' in new form. (Sales-folk would recognise this as the actual moment of sale.)

- *During 95-100%*: final resolution – 'return with the elixir'

The first half of the final-resolution is for the protagonist to know that the quest is over; the second half here is often a more public acknowledgement of the fact – a recognition by others rather than solely by self. There's often an explicit choice as to return back to the 'ordinary world' of the start, or to remain in the 'special world' defined by the story; and also usually some form of 'boon' or prize or reward at this point. (From a sales perspective, this is the key 'customer-satisfaction' moment.)

Once that 'return with the elixir' is complete, the ending needs to come as quickly yet cleanly as possible: it's all over bar the wrap-up and, of course, a setup for a possible sequel (otherwise known in the sales-context as 'repeat custom' – a point we'll probably return to later).

So that's the Hero's Journey story-pattern. It might sound a bit alien at first, but if we look around with our eyes attuned, we'll see that pattern surprisingly often in business: it matches well with many sales-processes, for example, as can be seen above.

And each traverse through a business-process is a self-contained story with its own actors, actions and events: we'll often find that some form of the Hero's Journey pattern fits well in those contexts too.

Where it *doesn't* fit so well is at the larger scale, for the enterprise as a whole, and especially so over the longer-term. The reason for this is to do with the overall nature of the story: single-shot, sequel, series or serial.

Most conventional films frame their stories as *single-shot* or *sequel*:

- A **single-shot story** is a once-off, typically in some form of Hero's Journey structure, with an emphasis on achieving a single goal or change.

I haven't seen many equivalents of this in the enterprise-context: a grand objective such as 'First Man On The Moon' or 'Eradicate Malaria' might seem to fit, but the respective organisation usually continues on in some form once the objective is achieved, and in fact is at risk of literally 'losing its story' if it aligns itself too strongly with the objective.

- A *sequel* is a once-off story, repeated, often without the emotive drivers that underpinned the original story.

In an enterprise-context, the sequels to 'First Man On The Moon' provide a well-known example: the energy and purpose of the NASA story there seemed all but lost, other than the unintended genre-shift to 'thriller' with Apollo 13...

By contrast, most enterprise-stories are more likely to take the form of a TV-style *series* or *serial*:

- A *series* is a set of similar episodes in much the same contextual space, and often with some of the same lead-players, yet also often not much direct connection between the episodes themselves.
- A *serial* has a set of repeated patterns that provide a strong continuity, chaining all the episodes together into a single 'grand story'.

A project-oriented organisation or consultancy will tend to look like a series-type story; a production-oriented organisation will tend to follow a serial-type enterprise-story.

A series can be quite fragmented, but a serial *must* take a long-term view: if it doesn't maintain that constant continuity, we risk ending up with a disjointed mess that doesn't make business sense – which is not a good idea.

So whilst the Hero's Journey type of story-structure often helps us make sense of a sales-process or business-process or a linear 'one-shot' project, it doesn't work so well for iterative stories, such as a series, or where many different stories weave through each other, such as in a serial. At the larger scale, we need a different type of story-structure – which is what we'll turn to next.

Application

- If your enterprise was a film, which film would it be? What film-genre would it fit best – a detective-story, a romantic-comedy, a disaster-movie? Who would you place as the lead-actors? And why?
- "Taut; elegant; spare: those are some of the words that we might use to describe a great screenplay." If your organisation's current architecture was a screenplay, what

adjectives would you use to describe it? How well does that screenplay hold the essence of your enterprise-story?

- Rather than what film it most resembles right now, which film *should* it be? What's the difference? To make that happen, what would need to change in that story you see right now?

- Your enterprise too will likely be "a huge collaborative effort", with many different skills and viewpoints brought to bear upon it. Who are all those people, these characters or stakeholders? What views and skills do they each bring to the story? What's needed to bring out the best from each, and maintain the balance between them to create a story that is a seamless, meaningful, unified whole?

- Where do you see hints of the Hero's Journey story-pattern play out within your own enterprise? Where do you *not* see that pattern? What are the key differences between those contexts, where you see that pattern, and where you don't?

- Is your organisation's story more a single-shot, a sequel, a series, or a serial? Why would you say this? What are the characteristics you see in your enterprise that would suggest to frame that story in one way rather than another?

INTERLUDE

Start work on this again this morning, yet again with a flood of new ideas, about storymind and storyworld, about storytelling and storylistening, about the relationships between character and culture, and a whole lot more.

None of which will fit at this point in the story.

Somehow I have to remember them all, keep them safe, ready to bring them back in when I *do* find their proper place in the story. Yet story is like that: the *telling* of the story may appear to be a nice, neat linear sequence – especially in hindsight – but it's often anything but linear when we're *within* the story itself. Tricky…

And then, moments later, that flood of ideas not only stops, but vanishes. Gone. A sense of flatness, nothingness, lostness; a sense of failure, almost. I don't know what to do… what do I do now? How can I recapture what just went past? How do I keep control of the story?

One of the hardest parts of the work of enterprise-architecture – especially when working with story – is that there *is* no control: 'control' is a myth, a fantasy, a delusion. Like story, it has its own time, which may not easily connect with ours. And it has its own imperatives, too, which likewise may conflict with ours. *Definitely* tricky there…

Application

- How do you capture ideas and images as they fly past in the moment? How do you find them again when you discover a place where they *do* fit within your enterprise-story? And how *do* you discover that 'right place' within the story?
- How do you cope with the 'need' for control of something that, almost by definition, is beyond any normal sense of control? How do you deal with *others'* need for you to seem to be in control of the story, or their need to be in 'control' of you in control of that story? What is it that *actually* holds the story together?

05: CIRCULAR STORIES

What kind of story-structure works best at the larger scale? If the Hero's Journey pattern is problematic here – because once we've achieved the goal, there's no more story – then what *do* we use?

For me, working with many different types of organisations over the past few decades, the answer seems to come in three distinct yet interleaved parts:

- the Story-Cycle
- the Strategy-Cycle
- the Market-Cycle

I'll describe each of those in turn, and how they interact, but perhaps not all of them in the one go.

Where this story starts is a long time ago – perhaps half a century or more? – with a man named Bruce Tuckman. He'd been trying to find a way to describe the sequence of activities in projects that succeed – and, equally, what happens in projects that don't. In particular, he recognised the importance of the people-issues, the 'group dynamics' in the lifecycle-story of the project.

And whilst the Hero's Journey does sort-of fit, the big difference is that projects are usually *collective*: it's more like an ensemble play than a follow-the-hero Hollywood movie. What Tuckman noticed was that whilst everyone seems to want to rush in and get started straight away as soon as there's the first glimmering of a new idea, there are two crucial intermediate stages that have to happen first. And they have to happen in the right order, too. So here was his first version of that sequence:

- *Forming* – we develop the idea, intent and aim for the project
- *Storming* – we find the right people for the project, and deal with the interpersonal issues that invariably arise
- *Norming* – we settle down to do planning and preparation
- *Performing* – we do the work to deliver the project

If we skip the Forming stage, we end up with literally aimless action, 'doing for the sake of doing'. Not a good idea – especially in a business context.

If we skip the Storming stage, the project is likely to collapse in a squabbling heap right at the critical point – and it won't recover. Many people do find it difficult to deal with the sheer *messiness* of all the interpersonal stuff, but it *is* part of the work, whether we like it or not – and the project won't succeed without it.

And if we skip the Norming stage, we'll cripple the Performing stage, because the things that we need will turn up in the wrong place, at the wrong time, be the wrong things, or be missing entirely. Whilst it's true that in many current project-contexts "no plan survives first contact with reality" (to paraphrase that old military dictum), we still need *some* form of plan – or plan*ning* – to ensure that we do have what we need when we need it.

Anyway, that's the core sequence for the project story: Forming, Storming, Norming, Performing.

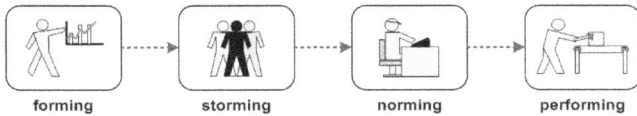

Figure 1: Tuckman sequence - linear

Yet whilst that story-structure makes sense for a single project, as viewed only in isolation, it's not quite complete in terms of what happens as one project ends and another begins. To deal with this, Tuckman added a final stage to the story-structure:

- *Adjourning* (or Mourning): we do an explicit completions and wrap-up for the project, including capture of lessons-learned

This then becomes a literal life-*cycle*, with the Adjourning of one project leading into and supporting the Forming of the next.

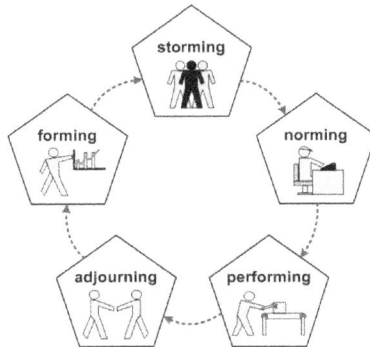

Figure 2: Tuckman sequence - cyclic

It's also a cycle that works in many different contexts – not just with projects or project-management – and at many different levels. To make the structure more generic, and to indicate that at the larger scale the stages may be handled by different parts of the organisation, I often use a different set of labels for this: Purpose, People, Preparation, Process, Performance. In essence, though, it's the same overall structure as in Tuckman's Group Dynamics.

Figure 3: Five Elements cycle

Each area of emphasis also has a different *time*-perspective:

- *Purpose*: far-future
- *People*: 'people-time' or 'story-time' – anywhen from far-past to far-future, and from no-time to any-time
- *Preparation*: near-future
- *Process*: NOW!
- *Performance*: past

One of the concerns highlighted here is that it can be hard to link between Performance and Purpose, to close the cycle, because Purpose looks far into the future, whilst Performance looks only to the past. It's the one place in the cycle where there's such an extreme difference in time-perspective: and the problems can be hard to spot *because* it's at the apparent end of the sequence.

We do see similar mismatches of perspective, though, when we reframe this as the Strategy-Cycle, linking between strategy, tactics and execution. The Purpose and People phases focus more on 'feel'; Preparation and Performance alike focus on thinking, planning, analysis; whilst Process, of course, will focus most on the practice, the 'doing'. In most business-contexts, people tend to be very strong on the thinking and the doing, but often not at all comfortable with feeling – which can lead to serious plot-holes in

30

the respective enterprise-story. But that's something we'll come back to later.

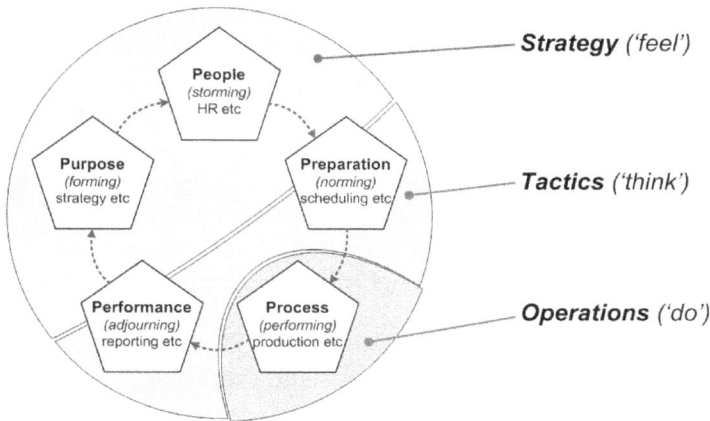

Figure 4: Strategy-cycle

This overall story-structure links well with cycles for continuous-learning, such as Deming and Shewhart's PDCA (Plan, Do, Check, Act), whose Check phase aligns with Tuckman's Adjourning stage – though that's probably a separate story to here.

The Tuckman cycle also aligns almost perfectly with the classic Chinese *wu xing* or Five Element structure (Wood, Fire, Earth, Metal, Water). A lot of useful insights to be gained from the analogy – though that too is probably another story for elsewhen.

What *does* matter here, though, is the different kinds of leadership that drive the story forward. We not only need leadership to guide *within* each stage, we also need leadership to link from one stage to the next. And importantly, these are *different types of leadership*, requiring different skillsets, and hence often different people as the respective leader for each phase.

This means that our equivalent of the Hero's Journey here will need another set of phases, *between* each of the Tuckman-style stages in the story-lifecycle. For this I use an adaptation of Nigel Green's VPEC-T (Values, Policies, Event, Content, Trust): the original was about exchanges between entities, but reframing its core ideas in terms of lifecycles also works well. The difference is that a focus on Content is less relevant for *this* purpose, because it's implied everywhere, especially as part of the Process stage; instead, we need Completions, to mark the end-events of Process, and link to the next stage, to assess Performance.

Which, overall, gives us an enterprise-scope Story-Cycle, that's also linked to the Strategy-Cycle:

- *Purpose* ['feel']: we develop the idea, intent and aim for the work – the *vision* for the work, and its expression as strategy
- *Values* ['feel']: we use vision and values embedded in the purpose to engage people's commitment to that purpose and strategy
- *People* ['feel']: we find the right people for the work, and deal with the interpersonal issues that invariably arise
- *Policies* [from 'feel' to 'think']: out of the discussion and arguments, we bring a framework for a plan and outline of tactics
- *Preparation* ['think']: we do all the planning and logistics needed to bridge between tactics and execution
- *Events* [from 'think' to 'do']: we await the trigger-event, the 'call to action'
- *Process* ['do']: we do the work to deliver the project
- *Completions* [from 'do' to 'think']: we note and act on the end-events that mark the call to *cease* action
- *Performance* ['think']: we do an explicit completions and wrap-up for the project, including capture of lessons-learned
- *Trust* [from 'think' to 'feel']: we connect the lessons-learned back to the initial aim and intent
- (and back to *Purpose* for the next iteration)

Or, in visual form:

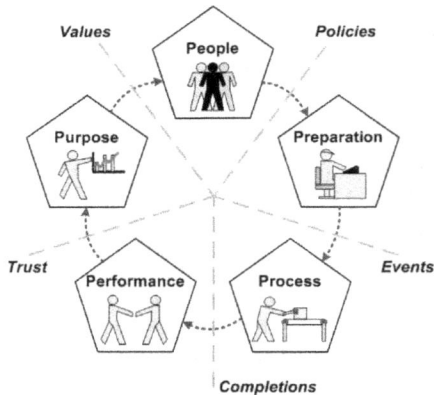

Figure 5: Story-cycle

There's one more type of leadership that's needed here, though it isn't part of the Story-Cycle itself: namely, the leadership needed to *hold the balance*. Another point we'll see again later, perhaps.

But right now, that's more than enough about the structure of story: this is supposed to be about story itself, after all. Time to heed that 'call to action', and move more into enterprise *as* story.

Application

- In your organisation's projects, where do you see examples of where Tuckman's sequence has *not* been followed: those five stages of Forming, Storming, Norming, Performing and Adjourning either occurring out of sequence, or skipped entirely? What are the consequences when this occurs?
- What methods are used within your organisation to capture and apply lessons-learned from projects? Within your organisation and your architecture, how do you link one project to the next? What are the stories here?
- At the larger scale, which parts of your organisation specialise in Purpose? (Strategy, for example?) Which parts emphasise the People-issues? Preparation? Process, or production? The tracking of Performance, and lessons-learned? Who leads each of these areas of the organisation?
- Which parts of your organisation link *between* each of those specialist emphases? Who leads that linking between areas, and how?
- What issues arise for your organisation because different areas have different time-perspectives? In what ways can you use architecture, and story-as-architecture, to bridge across those different worldviews?
- What happens to the balance of the whole when one area dominates over all the others? What can you do in *architectural* terms to bring the overall story back into balance?
- What do you see when you apply the Strategy-Cycle and Story-Cycle to example areas of your organisation? What's missing? Which stages are being skipped, or scrambled? In what stages of the cycle are there mixed-up mixes of 'feel', 'think' and 'do'? What are the consequences when this happens? And what can you do in *architectural* terms, with structure or with story, to bring it into better balance?

INTERLUDE

It's turned up twice now in the past couple of days, and a fair few times before that as well, so I guess I'd better pay attention to the formal theory on 'narrative-paradigm'.

The core of this comes from an academic named Walter Fisher, back in the 1980s. He suggested that most decision-makers in business and elsewhere held to a set of assumptions that could be described as the *rational-world paradigm*:

- people are essentially rational;
- rational argument is the key driver for decision-making and for communicating those choices and decisions;
- each formal discipline has its own distinct and different rules;
- the value of the reasoning is determined by subject-matter knowledge, and by ability to present, advocate for and defend a nominally-factual position;
- the world is a set of logical puzzles that can each be solved through analysis and reason.

It's from this that we get the cult of the 'expert', the cult of the MBA, the cult of 'just give me the numbers, give me the facts'. The catch is that this *only* works well when everything stays essentially the same, when we have the leisure and the certainty to optimise our 'rational-world' one factor at a time. It tends to fall apart as soon as it faces any kind of 'wicked problem', or anything else that's inherently indefinable or uncertain. Which means that it actually *doesn't* work well for much of what we face in enterprise architecture right now.

What works instead, said Fisher, is to acknowledge that people engage with ideas and with each other via *stories*. Hence what he described as the *narrative-paradigm*:

- people are essentially storytellers;
- 'good reasons' provide the key driver for decision-making and for communicating those choices and decisions;
- 'good reasons' are influenced by history, biography, culture, and character;

- the value of the reasoning is determined by narrative coherence, narrative probability and narrative fidelity;
- the world is a set of stories from which people choose.

Perhaps the key point here is that human decisions are ultimately *emotional* – not 'rational'. Formal reason, logic and fact will all play their part *before* the decision, and after it, too; but not *at* the actual moment of decision – a distinction that is extremely important in practice. So to be effective, even logic and rational argument must usually take a narrative form. Hence, in this case, the importance of story and narrative in enterprise-architecture.

The experience of the 'subject-matter expert' still has an important role, but in a sense it becomes subordinate to the story, rather than a would-be substitute for it:

> Intellectuals or experts serve best as counselors not tellers of 'a story that ends all storytelling.' To be effective, experts must make themselves subject to the demands of narrative rationality.

What Fisher describes as 'good reasons' are "inexplicably bound to a value, to a conception of the good" – 'good' in a social and moral sense, rather than solely in terms of some purported 'truth':

> Good reasons are rooted in fact, they are relevant to the issue at hand, they are tied to positive consequences, they conform to the life experience of the audience, and they plug into transcendent value – the highest good an individual can imagine.

Whether we like it or not, this kind of narrative-rationality *is* what drives any *human* enterprise. So to make our architecture work – to make it 'make sense', and to engage people in its intended outcomes – we cannot simply ignore narrative or story: we must work *with* it, and with its sometimes strange-seeming imperatives. This does have real advantages too, though, because it can make some aspects of the work very much easier:

> We are able to communicate across cultures, genders, races and epochs because our good reasons are communicated through narratives or stories that are universally intelligible. The operative principle of narrative rationality is identification rather than deliberation.

And as we already know from the existing architectural emphasis on views and viewpoints, our stories must also be shaped to fit the self-conception of each specific audience:

Any story, any form of rhetorical communication not only says something about the world, it also implies an audience, persons who conceive of themselves in very specific ways. If a story denies a person's self-conception, it does not matter what it says about the world. In the instance of protest, rival factions' stories deny each other in respect to self-conceptions and the world. The only way to bridge this gap, if it can be bridged through discourse, is by telling stories that do not negate the self-conceptions that people hold of themselves.

There are facts we need to work with in our architecture, of course – a myriad of facts. Yet in what Fisher suggests above, ultimately *the enterprise is a story.* How we deal with that fact is up to us…

Application

- "The world is made of puzzles to be solved", or "the world is made of stories": which of those two assertions rings more true for you? Which groups amongst your architecture-stakeholders would gravitate more to the 'rational-world paradigm'? Which groups more to the 'narrative paradigm'?

- In what ways do you adapt your existing architecture-narrative for each audience? What are the differences between the stories you tell to each stakeholder-group?

- "To be effective, experts must make themselves subject to the demands of narrative rationality": if that's true, and given the mindset and self-importance of many supposed 'experts', how would you entice them to 'make themselves subject' to the very different demands of story?

06: DEFINING THE STORY

Okay, so we know that we need to explore story in relation to enterprise-architecture. But *which* story? How do we identify that story? I know we're supposed to be working with story-as-story by now, but a bit more structure would certainly help…

At this point it might be useful to turn to Dramatica – a kind of screenwriter's equivalent of the Zachman framework, providing a 'taxonomy of story' that describes a *storymind* for the respective story. With only minor translation, much of this would sound very familiar to enterprise-architects:

> Every complete story is a model of the mind's problem
> solving process. To fully explore any issue, an author has to
> examine all possible solutions to that issue and make an
> argument to prove to an audience that the author's way is
> best.

> If you leave out a part of that argument or diverge from the
> point, your story will have plot holes or inconsistencies. Once
> you have covered every angle in your argument, you've
> mapped all the ways an audience might look at that problem
> and, therefore, all the ways anyone might look at that
> problem. In short, you have created a map of the mind's
> problem solving process.

> Characters, Plot, and Theme are the thoughts of this Story
> Mind made tangible. An audience can see them and learn.

Hence, in turn, the storymind for the storyworld of our enterprise-architecture.

Like Zachman, Dramatica is a bit mechanical in approach, and can sometimes leave us floundering in 'excruciating detail'. Yet unlike Zachman, Dramatica does provide both framework *and* process to develop characters and story. Although it's aimed at creation of narrative-style stories, some parts are also useful for exploring the backstory of an overall enterprise – and especially to identify the drivers for enterprise response to change and innovation.

The Dramatica process is based around twelve questions, ten of which are directly relevant to the 'storymind' that underpins an enterprise and its architecture. The first set of four questions relate directly to the overall story of the enterprise, with stakeholders as 'characters' within that shared story:

- *Overall Throughline*: If we look at the enterprise-story from a bird's eye view, which general area best describes the nature of the problems all the stakeholders are dealing with? Do the story's conflicts or tensions stem from a *Situation* (external state), an *Activity* (external process), a *Fixed Attitude* (internal state) or *Manipulations* (internal process)?
- *Overall Concern*: Which area of concern are all the stakeholders in the enterprise-story interested in or worried about regarding the overall enterprise vision or 'goal'?
- *Overall Issue*: What is the thematic issue that affects all of the stakeholders in the enterprise-story?
- *Overall Problem*: What is the source of the central problem that affects all the stakeholders in the enterprise-story?

Two of the questions focus more on the part (the Role) that the organisation chooses to play within the overall enterprise:

- *Story Driver*: Is the overall enterprise-story driven by *Actions* first, leading to decisions (reactive response to something happening – such as an emergency-response team) or *Decisions* first, leading to actions (proactive choice – such as a decision to develop a new product or service)?
- *Story Limit*: Is the overall enterprise-story constrained more by *Time* (delivery-driven – such as logistics) or by *Options* (investigation-driven – such as innovation, or legal enquiry)?

(The other two questions in that Dramatica set – 'Story Outcome' and 'Main Character Judgement' – are more related to the closure of a 'single-shot' narrative-story, and don't really apply to an ongoing story such as that of the enterprise.)

And the final four questions focus more on the organisation itself, as if it were the main-character in an ongoing story:

- *Organisation Resolve*: Does the organisation *Change* its way of dealing with the problem at the heart of the enterprise-story (adapting to the changes in market, perhaps), or remain *Steadfast* in its convictions (as an infrastructure-provider usually must)?
- *Organisation Growth* (in terms of character, not size): Does the organisation grow by adopting new useful traits (*Start*) or by outgrowing old inappropriate ones (*Stop*)?

- *Organisation Approach*: Is the organisation a *Be-er* that adapts to a changing environment or a *Do-er* that actively changes the business-environment?
- *Organisation Problem Solving Style*: Does the organisation emphasise a *Logical* problem-solving style (formal analysis, 'scientific') or an *Intuitive* problem-solving style (relational, holistic, 'design-thinking')?

There's a lot there that can be very useful in making sense of the enterprise-story – and of the architectural choices that we may have within it.

As we saw earlier, some parts of Hollywood-style story-structure – such as character-arc or story-mood – either don't fit with what we need, or at first may not seem to make much sense in our context. Yet there's still a lot there that does align well with our needs in architecture – another of which is *story-genre*.

Genre is a means to categorise stories in terms of particular 'rules' and expectations. For films, these include genres such as family-drama, thriller, science-fiction, romantic-comedy and suchlike. But these don't map directly to a business context: instead, we need genres that focus more on the overall aim or feel – and, again, the 'rules' and expectations for the respective business-story. So a more business-oriented set of genres might include these:

- *The Fixer* – typified by phrases such as "we take away the hassle" or "it just works"
- *We Sell Certainty* – banking, insurance, pharmaceutical and health-industries usually express this type of story
- *Everything You Need Is Here* – supermarkets, stores and shopping-malls tend to congregate around this type of story
- *You're Special...* – a common genre in the fashion, beauty, travel and hospitality industries, and in entertainment too
- *Life Is Exciting!* – gambling, racing and nightclubs are obvious examples of this, though also gadget-oriented technology-industries
- *Absurdistan* – a focus more on the quirky, the strange, the unexpected, as typified by much of the entertainment industry
- *Road Movie* – for obvious reasons, a genre that's popular with the travel and transport industries
- *The Explorers* – often associated with research and education, though also often in the arts as well

- *We're On Your Side* – an assertive 'us against them' story (sometimes in extreme form as 'Vengeance Shall Be Yours'), commonly associated with law, politics and the military
- *This Is Serious* – an enterprise equivalent of the investigative documentary, popular with politicians, activists and many non-government organisations

Each of these enterprise-genres has its own distinct 'rules': for example, in a The Fixer story, everything really *must* 'just work' and 'remove hassle', otherwise the story falls apart.

Attempts at mix-and-match of genres occur quite often in current films and TV-series: for example, a western-genre story set in the far reaches of outer space, or a teen-drama with horror-story elements – as in Joss Whedon's *Firefly* and *Buffy* respectively. How well this works in practice is always a moot point, but one of the key factors is that the resultant story must obey the 'rules' of *all* of the merged genres.

The same applies to business-stories. So if, like many shopping-malls, we aim to combine the story-genre of You're Special with that of Everything You Need Is Here, the former genre's sense of pampering and luxury has to carry through everything in *every* part of the mall; yet we'll also need a lot of variety and choice, to support the latter genre of 'everything you need'. And that's likely to be very expensive to set up and to maintain – which limits the story-options in different ways. Just as in films, a mixed-genre business-story can be a great way to differentiate from the 'me-too' crowd: but getting the right balance between the genres can be a lot harder than it looks – and if we don't get it right, the whole story breaks down. More on this later, probably.

Finally, another essential part of story-structure is the need to *establish the story*. In business terms, this is about explaining exactly what business we're in: what we do, what we don't do, who we are, why we're here.

As in Hollywood stories, the trick here is "show, don't tell": we don't drown people in the detail, we set the scene with subtle hints, and above all by action and by example. Branding is one obvious means to set the scene, but in an organisational context perhaps even more through consistent use of pattern, image and metaphor – hence the real importance of corporate-identity and the like, to establish the 'look and feel' of how our organisation relates to the overall enterprise.

Application

- Explore each of the Dramatica questions above, in the context of your own organisation and enterprise: what do you find? How would you apply what you find?

- What genre would apply best to your organisation's intended story? Looking around at other organisations and industries, what additional genres can you identify? What are the 'rules' that apply to each genre?

- In what ways, and to what extent, is each story a mix-and-match between genres? How well does the genre-mix work in each case?

- How would you establish the architectural story of your enterprise? Through what means can you apply the film-industry aphorism of "show, don't tell", to imply the enterprise context, the background, the deeper backstory? How do you ensure consistency of the story across the whole enterprise, whilst still allowing the story to be itself?

INTERLUDE

My colleague Peter Bakker sent this to me this evening:

The *'Keep It Simple' Storytelling for Architects* Manifesto:

We are uncovering better ways of developing architectures by doing it and helping others do it. Through this work we have come to value:

-- *Connecting people* over connecting things

-- *Storytelling* over complex frameworks, models and tools

-- *Architecture as an emergent property* over architecture as a possession

--*Interacting with change* over following rigid upfront designs and models

That is, whilst there is value in the items on the right, we value the items on the left more.

Yet another theme to to think about whilst I'm already struggling with all of this. Oh well. Seems relevant, though...

Application

- "Whilst there is value in the items on the right, we value the items on the left more": is that true for you? If so, why? If not, why not? What *do* you value more?

- If you were to write your own equivalent of this 'manifesto', what comparisons would it contain? What would be on the left, that you value more? What would be on the right, still of value but of lower priority? What are your reasons for this? Are those reasons in terms of a 'rational-world' paradigm, a 'narrative-world' paradigm, or what?

07: WHERE IS THE STORY?

Still moving slowly away from structure towards... *something*, anyway, even if I don't quite know what it is as yet...

This next part seems to be a pick-up from that starting-point about architecture as narrative:

> Architecture is a vehicle for the telling of stories, a canvas for relaying societal myths, a stage for the theater of everyday life.

What this seems to be saying is that the *structures* of architecture – our more usual view of enterprise-architecture so far – are what provide the 'stage' or backdrop for "the theater of everyday life", in the business sense. In other words, the *where* of the story.

In some ways there's a strange sort of inversion here: the stage, as the backdrop for the story, is a structure, whereas story has its own form of truth – as would be clear from that notion of the storymind and its expression in genre and the like. Yet there are also some important parallels here to the relationships between a story and the structures of the theatre on which, and through which, that story is enacted. In effect, the theatre is the *medium* for the story – and as in Marshall McLuhan's oft-quoted phrase, the medium itself is part of the message. The *channels* through the organisation interacts with the broader enterprise are a key part of its message, its part in the shared story of the enterprise.

Another important paradox here is the way in which – in terms of architecture, anyway – we would often want to flaunt and show off the shape and structure of our theatre; but as soon as the show is running, we want the theatre itself to all but disappear from awareness, leaving only the story in view. In a business sense, the system often succeeds most to the extent that we *don't* see it. And it takes an enormous amount of skill and effort 'behind the scenes' to make it disappear that well, too.

One more useful architectural metaphor here is the late-mediaeval concept and practice of 'memory-theatre' – using the design and layout of structures themselves to help anchor the story, and to propel it forward. This part of architecture seems almost forgotten now: compare the richness of a Victorian theatre-auditorium or an Art Deco cinema with the grey utilitarian blandness of a modern multiplex. But in the past, the structure itself was part of the story: images and icons scattered throughout the space helped actors to memorise their lines, and the props also often supported the same practical purpose. Mediaeval churches were much the same, too: brightly-coloured, rich in imagery and symbolism, structure *as* story. There's a lot we could learn from formal research on this, such as in Frances Yates' classic *The Art of Memory*, or, in a more abstract and more structural form, the architectural-patterns in Christopher Alexander's *A Pattern Language*.

It's also worthwhile to make a habit out of repeatedly asking that one simple question *'Where's the story?'*. The reality is that story is *everywhere* in enterprise-architecture, as can be seen straight away once we learn how and where to look – and once we remember, too, that story is always in some way about *people*. For example:

- *process-volume* – where are these processes? Who is affected by each process? In what ways are they affected by varying process-volumes? Who is responsible for each aspect of the process, and for managing variance of volume?

- *capability-development* – where are these capabilities needed? What level of skill is required in each case? Where the capability is applied directly by people, how and where will they develop these capabilities? Where the capability is embedded in machines or IT-systems, who is responsible for developing and maintaining that capability? Where and how is each aspect of that story developed?

- *business-scenario* – where, when, how and to whom would this scenario apply? Who is responsible for enacting the scenario, or for developing and validating the scenario, and where would they do this?

- *use-case* – where, when and with whom would this use-case apply? Who is responsible for enacting the use-case, and with which systems? Who is responsible for defining, developing and validating the use-case, and where would they do this?

- *resource-management* – where are these resources? Where do they need to be, and in what ways do they need to be managed? Who will manage those resources, where, and using what capabilities? Who is responsible for each aspect of resource-management, at each type of location?

- *exchange-protocol* – what is exchanged, where, and under which rules? Who is responsible for each exchange, and for the rules and stories that govern each exchange?

44

- *transaction* – what is each transaction, and where does it take place? What events mark the start and end of each transaction, and where do those events take place? If the transaction takes place only between machines or IT-systems, who is responsible for ensuring that those transactions are appropriately monitored, and for taking appropriate action if and when they fail? Where are such responsibilities enacted, using what structures?

- *governance* – to what does the governance apply, and where? Who is responsible for that each aspect of that governance – including governance of the governance itself? Through which structures is this governance applied, and where?

- *system-overload* – where in the overall architecture can overload occur? What and who would be affected by each instance of overload? What impact will this have on each person's story, or their engagement in the enterprise-story? Who is responsible for resolving each overload, for identifying potential overload or risk of overload, and where within the structures would such work take place?

- *standards* – what standards apply throughout the architecture, and where? Who is responsible for ensuring that each standard is applied appropriately, and where and in what forms does such validation take place?

- *risks* – what risks apply throughout the architecture, and where do they apply? How do these risks change over time, in different contexts, in different locations, and in different types of locations? Who is responsible for evaluating such risks, for mitigating the risks, and for resolving the outcomes if the risks do eventuate? Where within the structures and the story of the architecture would these responsibilities apply?

- *customer-experience* – where and how does each customer experience each aspect of the architecture's structures and stories? Within the organisation's structures, who is responsible for monitoring each experience, and ensuring appropriate outcomes? Where does such monitoring and response take place?

- *customer-journey* – where does this 'journey' start? Where does it end? What and where are the various touchpoints along the way? Which structures and other architectural features are used or accessed within each journey? In what ways does the story weave through all these various places, for whom, and with whom?

In short, we combine *What's the story?* with *Where's the story?*, in relation to the architecture – and watch the insights arise…

Application

- What are the channels through which your organisation connects with the broader enterprise? In what ways do these affect how the organisation's own story can be told? If the channels themselves distort the overall story, through what architectural options can you change this, to create a smoother flow for the story?

- What parts of your 'theatre' do you want on show? What parts should always stay 'behind the scenes'? And how do you make even the 'on-show' parts of the theatre disappear from view once the story really starts?

- In what ways can you use the patterns and structures of your architecture to provide a kind of active-mnemonic to support the story? Exploring standard texts such as *The Art of Memory* or *A Pattern Language*, what do you discover there that can help you in this?

- Exploring those questions above, associated with the question 'Where's the story?', what do you learn from this? What other 'where'-questions arise as you do this? In what ways can you use story, and the 'where' of story, to engage people more in the intent and purpose and responsibilities of the architecture?

08: WHEN IS THE STORY?

"What's the first rule of comedy? – Timing!" And much the same is true for enterprise-stories: perhaps not quite "it's all in the timing", but close enough. In that sense, timing and pacing are the 'when' of the enterprise-story.

Timing is often the hidden-nightmare of enterprise-architecture. Just-in-time no-inventory systems sound great until there's a fuel-strike, a fire at a supplier's factory, or an earthquake on the far side of the world – and then suddenly the whole supply-chain will grind to a halt for the want of one single key component. And then there's the classic 'deadly-embrace' problem in resource-allocation: one process locks the disk and then asks for the printer, whilst another process locks the printer and asks for the disk, with the result that both processes are stuck waiting for the other to get started. All real-world systems are riddled with parallel-process problems such as these.

Synchronisation issues can be problematic enough, but tracking problems in asynchronous systems can be a whole lot harder, especially over longer timescales. At one of my clients, it took quite a while before anyone realised that all the work of the data-quality team – all that tedious effort of cleaning up garbled or out-of-date addresses – was being wiped out each weekend by a long-forgotten but still-active batch-update from an old and redundant database. No shortage of other examples there…

These timing-issues and missed connections add a whole layer of additional complexity to already-complex interdependencies of systems. And often the only way to make sense of them – or even to find them in the first place – is through story: follow the path, follow the sequence, "this happens, and then this happens, and then that happens too".

We also need to align 'when' with 'who' – especially where the process connects up with someone or something beyond our own organisation, and hence beyond our nominal 'control'. And where real-people are involved, we also need to be aware of expectations about time, and timing: no-one much minds if a hole-in-the-wall cash-machine takes an extra second or so to respond to a balance-request at busy times, but one of the best ways to *really* annoy a customers is to keep them trapped in a queuing-system that keeps them on hold for half an hour or more, blurting out a mechanical 'your-call-is-important-to-us' exactly once each minute whilst the wait drags on and on. A story there that we most definitely dare not ignore...

Pacing and *rhythm* are other aspects of story that apply equally to organisations. Each genre will have its own rules about pace and timing, yet also about rhythm and variation of pace too: even a fast-paced thriller will have its quiet moments, if only as 'the calm before the storm'.

In the same way, a fast-paced enterprise will still need its own quiet-times, places within time or space or both to pull back for a moment, to reflect, to learn. And if there's no change in pace at all and everything is rushed and blurred together without any gap or letup or break or anything where we might get any kind of chance to catch our breath and before we know it the next task has come through and we have to deal with it straight away and the next and the next and then the next is even worse and we haven't had a hope of fixing what went wrong in that before there's yet another disaster coming down the line you can see it's not surprising if things tend to break under that kind of stress is it?

Sigh...

And then there's the opposite, where nothing much happens.

Or *nothing* happens.

And we wait.

And wait.

And wait.

For something.

To start.

Or stop.

Or *something*.

Possibly.

If we knew what it was.

But no-one bothers to tell us.

And we don't know.

So we wait.

And wait.

Again.

Which has its own stresses, too. Perhaps worse than the over-paced enterprise, because the stress is in the wait itself. We know that something *should* happen, and that we need to respond to it as soon as it does; but we may not even know what it is that we're waiting for, or why we're waiting for it. That's hard.

So a real part of enterprise-architecture here is about creating the right balance of time and pace in the story. A sprint has its own fast pace: but most organisations are more like a marathon, a relay-race, a series or serial of a story that continues on and on. So sometimes it's short, sharp, staccato. And then there's time for a breath, and more than a breath, and it slows, to a smooth sonorous silence; and back to pick up the pace, and perhaps the pieces too, get everything back in its place before the next onslaught arrives, and fast, and fast again. Movement and rest, rest and movement, like breathing; that's how a story moves. Hence likewise with the enterprise. And, in turn, its architecture.

Timing and pace: key aspects of the enterprise story.

Yet whose story *is* it, anyway? Who owns the enterprise? That too is often not as simple as it seems – and another key aspect of this story that we need to explore...

Application

- What timing-issues do you see across your enterprise? Which parts don't line up in their timing? What are the respective timescales? What's the story in each case?

- What happens when timing goes wrong? Who is affected in each case? What impact does it have on their story?

- What is the pacing of your enterprise? What are its rhythms, its patterns in time? In what ways do these vary across different parts of the enterprise? In what ways do the patterns themselves vary over time – the rhythm of the rhythm itself?

09: WHOSE STORY?

Whose story *are* we dealing with here? The short answer is that it's the story of everyone in the enterprise: but this is where things tend to get a bit messy in most current enterprise-architecture...

An architecture will typically describe structures of some kind. And, as the term suggests, all of enterprise-architecture is about the architecture of the enterprise: no surprises there, I'd imagine? Yet something that evidently confuses a lot of people is that often it's not all that much about the organisation itself: it's much more about how the organisation relates with its chosen enterprise. And the key to this is that *organisation and enterprise are not the same.*

There are some fundamental distinctions here that we must not ignore – otherwise we risk working on entirely the wrong story. Perhaps the best illustration is a phrase from 1930s economist John Maynard Keynes, about 'the animal spirits of the entrepreneur' – which is probably not how we'd describe most organisations? So the simplest way to summarise the distinctions is that:

- an ***organisation*** is bounded by *rules, roles* and *responsibilities* – a *conceptual* and *practical* construct
- an ***enterprise*** is bounded by *vision, values* and *commitments* – an *emotive* and *aspirational* construct

The organisation is more conceptual or practical, the *How* and *With-What* of what we do. But the enterprise is about emotion, aspirations, drive: it's the *Why* for whatever we choose to do. If we focus too much on the organisation – the How and With-What – it becomes all too easy to forget about the Why, the reasons why and with-whom and for-whom we're doing all of this in the first place. We *need* to be clear about those distinctions.

In the context of story, we could put it another way:

- *organisation* aligns with *structure* – in fact *is* structure
- *enterprise* aligns with *story* – in fact *is* a story

Hence, for the architecture to work, we need the right balance of structure and story, organisation and enterprise. We create our architecture *for* an organisation, *about* the enterprise within which that organisation operates; the enterprise defines the *context* for the organisation's *content*. All of these distinctions are crucial for the foundations of a viable enterprise-architecture.

One of the most useful guidelines is that the enterprise-in-scope – '*the* enterprise', for our enterprise-architecture – should be three steps larger than the organisation-in-scope – the organisation for which we're developing that architecture. To illustrate this, let's start with the common assumption that the organisation 'is' the enterprise:

Figure 6: Organisation as enterprise-in-scope

The catch here is that if the organisation says it 'is' the enterprise, it in effect declares that its only interest is literally self-centred. Its 'Why' is so focussed on itself that there's no real reason for anyone else to want or need connect with it: there's no shared-story - and hence, often, no story at all.

In practice, the minimum real enterprise is the *immediate supply-chain* – a story of shared *transactions*:

Figure 7: Immediate supply-chain as enterprise-in-scope

At the very least, this story extends outward from the organisation to supplier on one side and customers on the other. In practice, the scope we need to take into account for the enterprise-architecture here would cover a fair-sized value-web, from supplier's supplier to customer's customer – as per the SCOR supply-chain standard – including all manner of alternate-parties on either side. It's wise to assess this in symmetrical form, not least because a business-model can be made or broken as easily on the supply-side as on the customer-side.

One essential point on governance to note here: *the classic concepts of 'command-and-control' cannot and do not apply to any part of the enterprise beyond the borders of the organisation.* By definition, the boundary of the organisation *is* the boundary of control. Beyond that point, everything depends on negotiation, agreement, trust: in other words, not on would-be 'control', but on the shared-story – and the 'sharedness' of that story, too.

To support that shared-story, the next step outward is the *market* – a broader enterprise of *potential or abstract transactions*:

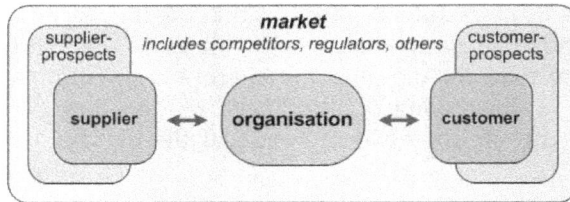

Figure 8: Market as enterprise-in-scope

This broader scope includes all potential customers and suppliers, all actual and potential competitors, and so on. It also includes players such as regulators, analysts and infrastructure-providers, whose services help to define the overall market itself, as a 'meta-organisation' with its own shared rules, roles and responsibilities.

And then there's another distinct layer beyond the market, which we might describe as the 'extended-enterprise':

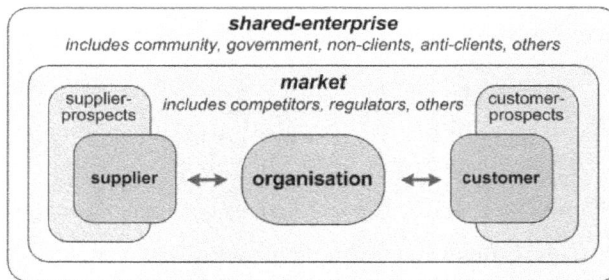

Figure 9: Extended-enterprise as enterprise-in-scope

These people may not have any direct transactions as such with the organisation – or even the market as a whole – but are affected by it and can affect it in turn. In that sense, they are *stakeholders* in the overall enterprise – and can and will hold the organisation to account in terms of the vision, values and commitments implied by that shared-enterprise. These stakeholders will often include:

- *families* and *communities* of employees, customers and suppliers, and others affected in turn by *their* employees and the like
- *governments* at the various local, regional and national levels, concerned about tax-bases, infrastructure-provision and so on

- *non-clients* who may have an interest in the enterprise but are not able or are no longer able or willing to be active players within it
- *anti-clients* who often share a strong commitment to the enterprise, but also strongly disagree with the way the organisation or even the entire market relate to that enterprise

(We'll come back later to the question of anti-clients, and how a story-based approach can help us understand what to do there.)

The same pattern extends further, of course – at the larger scope we'll often notice an 'enterprise of enterprises' – but the three-step above is usually all we'll need to deal with directly.

Anyway, that's the real scale of the scope that we need to address when we talk about 'the enterprise'. Its actual scope will vary, of course, dependent on what we use as our starting-point, our 'the organisation': if we start from the business as a whole, we'd likely end up with a scope much as above, but if we were to start solely from within IT, our 'extended-enterprise' would be the broader business-organisation, much as described in TOGAF and the like. The important point, though, is that are a *lot* of stakeholder-groups in any real enterprise-architecture – and we need to take account of all of them within the enterprise-story.

What all of this tells us is two distinct themes.

One is that we must create the architecture around this broader shared-story – not solely around our organisation's structures.

The other is that we probably need to think much more carefully about what may be, to many people, a really worrying question: if every one of those stakeholders has a stake in the enterprise-story, *who owns the enterprise*? Once again, the answer is not as simple as it looks – and, not as simple as it's seemed in the past…

More on that in a moment, anyway.

Application

- Before reading this chapter, would you have said that the organisation and the enterprise were essentially the same? What difference does it make to your architecture if you start to view them as different, in the sense described here?
- What's the 'boundary of control' for your organisation and for your architecture? Within that architecture and its governance, how do you deal with issues such as exchange-

protocols and other partner-relationships that cross that boundary of control?

- Given that three-step structure, who are the suppliers and customer and other partners – the first enterprise-step outward – that you need to acknowledge within your architecture? What are the interfaces, the transactions and other interactions? How do you model each of these within the architecture?

- The next step outward is indirect-connections and proto-interactions – market-definition, market-governance, prospects, competitors and the like. Who are they? What are these interactions, or information-gathering exercises? If at all, how do you model each of these within the architecture?

- The third step outward is the often seemingly-distant interactions with families, communities, government, non-clients and anti-clients? Who are these stakeholder-groups? What impact does your organisation have on these groups? What impact can they have on your organisation? How, if at all, do you model each of these within the architecture?

- What are the common threads that link each of these groups together? What *is* 'the enterprise' – the storyworld – within which every one of them is a stakeholder? What's the unifying story of this shared-enterprise?

10: WHO OWNS THE STORY?

The enterprise-story is where people connect with the enterprise. It's also *how* they connect with the enterprise: each person in the enterprise *commits to* and *participates in* the enterprise-story, in their own unique way, if only as a side-effect of engagement in the enterprise and its story. This is what makes marketing possible: marketers create a story that in some way relates to the story of the overall enterprise, to open the way for a connection with the organisation.

Yet if the enterprise-story defines the enterprise, who owns the story?

In the past there's been a simple answer to that question: the organisation owns the story. Or *possesses* the story, rather. The story as trademark, as brand, as private property. The story told only as a one-way broadcast from the marketing department, the PR department, through channels that the organisation also exclusively controls and owns.

Over the past decades, the marketplace itself has been changed from a public space – the muddled yet so *human* chaos of the street-market or the town square – to a controlled, filtered, private possession – the medium is the message is the mall. Even the ancient shared stories have become private property: Disney owns Snow White, Cinderella, the Beauty and the Beast. Ferrari owns the colour red; Harley-Davidson the sound of an engine; a small Australian telco even claims to own the word 'Yes'.

And if the organisation seems to own the story, it's easy to believe that the organisation *is* the enterprise, the enterprise *is* the organisation. Given enough cash, clout and coercion, a company could easily delude itself into thinking that it has the power and the right to control the story – or at least to silence every other version of that story.

The company's story drowns out all other voices, other stories, is everything, everywhere, for everyone: all-pervading, ubiquitous, inevitable – with no place and no permission for any other story to exist. Enterprise-story as privileged possession, the possession of the privileged.

Which leads, in turn, to the ubiquity of the demand that we stay 'on message'. HR Department and PR Department as thought-police, ever watchful for signs of 'thoughtcrime', the literal heresy of 'thinking otherwise': every employee's weblog must carry some disclaimer such as "The opinions expressed here are my own and not those of my employer". If we're allowed to have opinions of our own at all...

Command-and-control treats all others as subjects (command) or objects (control): and since to be a member of an organisation demands that we place ourselves subject to its rules, command-and-control of the message might seem to succeed here.

Yet there's a catch: *organisation and enterprise are not the same.*

We can control an organisation – in principle, at least – because it's bounded by its rules; but *we cannot control an enterprise*, because it's bounded not by rules but by shared commitment. That commitment is an outcome of emotion – and emotions are not subject to anyone's else's control. (How we *respond* to those emotions can be a choice, but not the emotions themselves.) And commitment to the enterprise only happens when the story is shared – which, by definition, cannot happen if only one version of the story is allowed, because there's no space in which to *share* the story.

Most people also don't respond well to command and coercion: they retreat back to their own story, offering only the absolute minimum of commitment needed to get by. Hence the more an organisation tries to control the story, the more it *prevents* engagement in its own enterprise.

Under those circumstances, clients can easily become anti-clients – with serious yet seemingly-unexpected impacts on the organis-ation. The only way forward is for the organisation to loosen its grip on the enterprise – in other words, to let go of its futile and often increasingly-desperate attempts to command and control.

Not that the organisation has all that much choice now, about relinquishing that control. Even a decade ago, mass-media still dominated the public thought-space; there were so few channels that it was still feasible for companies to seem to control the message, in a one-way broadcast from company to 'consumer'. The company might sometimes have had to shout louder and shout wider to ensure that the message came across, but that was about all that was needed: litigation and lawyers could easily demolish any remaining dissent.

Yet the combination of the internet and new media – especially on mobiles – has changed the game completely: the old mass-media are in danger of dying, as an infinity of new micro-channels open up, each with their own authoritative voice. Suddenly it's no longer one-to-many, but many-to-many-to-many – and even the most repressive of regimes are finding this new hydra-headed 'monster' all but impossible to control.

The new media also enable many-to-one messages, such that the organisation can sometimes even find its own voice swamped and silenced – a scary experience for some...

The organisation's anti-clients can now also wield every bit as much influence as the organisation itself. A single YouTube video such as Dave Carroll's all-too-literal 'smash-hit' song *United Breaks Guitars* might destroy many years'-worth of carefully-crafted corporate messages in a matter of minutes – and it barely counts at all as to whether or not the anti-client's complaint is 'fair' from the organisation's perspective.

One of Dave Snowden's dictums of knowledge-management is that sharing of knowledge cannot be coerced – it can only be volunteered. The same applies to attention and trust: they cannot be coerced. Instead, if we want to gain others' attention and trust, we have to create conditions under they *can* be volunteered. Which means that we need to let go of the story, and allow others' stories to meld into the broader story of the shared-enterprise.

What makes letting-go hard is the 'need' to possess the 'true version' of the story. Others' complaints about our organisation may seem 'unfair', for example – yet they *are* a real part of that story, and each provides its own thread to create a richer fabric of story.

Another reason why we need to understand the new media, in relation to the enterprise-story, is that it's through those many-to-many links that our anti-clients are most likely to connect with each other and with the wider community, and where 'anti-stories' about the enterprise will develop and spread. If we don't keep track of what's happening in that world, our own equivalent of 'United Breaks Guitars' will seem to arrive out of nowhere – catching us off-guard with nowhere to go. Being visible and available within these media gives us a place to engage with those stories at the earliest possible opportunity – and help bring them back to align with the overall enterprise-story.

Yet there's another important catch here too. The more we align with the enterprise-story and its underlying vision and values, the greater engagement we can gain from our stakeholders; but those other stakeholders will also hold us more accountable to that story, too.

Playing fast-and-loose with the story, or trying to rig it solely to our advantage over others, will be a very dangerous mistake. In the new internet age of immersive transparency, any perceived betrayal of the enterprise-story by the purported custodians of that story is probably the quickest way of all to create vast numbers of anti-clients – which can kill the company stone-dead in days if we're not very careful indeed. Responsibility *matters* here – our responsibilities to, with and for the enterprise-story.

The enterprise is a story. But the organisation is not the whole of the enterprise: it never was. And the organisation does not possess the story: it never did. How you deal with those facts, in your architecture and within your organisation, is up to you.

Application

- Who owns the story? Perhaps more to the point, who *believes* that they own the story, or have a 'right' to possess the story, even though in practice they don't? Conversely, what happens when *no-one* takes responsibility for the story?
- What attempts are made within your organisation to control the story? It's likely that some aspects of the story will be more rigidly 'controlled' than others: which aspects of the story, and why? What is it that drives that perceived 'need' for control? What's the story behind that story?
- What are the consequences, to the individual, to the organisation and to the enterprise as a whole, if someone fails to keep 'on message'? What are the consequences if someone *doesn't* break free from that controlled version of the story?

11: WHICH STORY?

We need the story: and, clearly, more than just the organisation's version of the story. Yet a random collection of themes and views is not a story: so how *do* we ensure that the threads do hold together into a unified, unifying vision for the enterprise? Not just whose story, but *which* story – that's the question here.

The conventional view of the enterprise-story is 'inside-out' – start from the organisation's viewpoint, and move outward from there. But as Chris Potts put it in his book *recrEAtion*, "Customer do not appear in our processes: *we* appear in their experiences". And if that's the case, we definitely need to balance that 'inside-out' view with 'outside-in' – a story of the enterprise as a whole, and where we fit within that story.

What's a real example to illustrate this? Well, one example we could use is Carnaval, in Rio de Janeiro. It only lasts a few days each year – in fact it's happening right now as I write this – but it's *huge*: a city-wide party for millions of people, around a quarter of a million people directly employed, an effective income overall of more than half a billion dollars. As an enterprise, parts of it extend throughout the year, and it affects the whole city and far beyond.

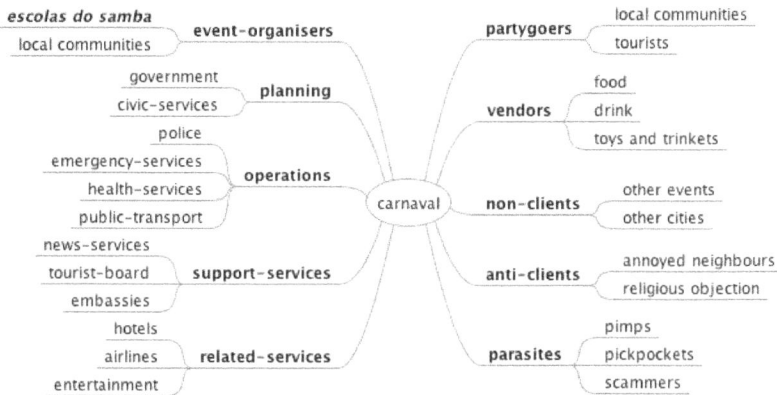

Figure 10: Carnaval – example stakeholders

That rough mind-map outlines some of the stakeholders in this enterprise-story. Many, many different groups and organisations, each with their own distinct view of the story – and all of them have a stake in whether the Carnaval story succeeds or fails. (Even the parasites from the grey-economy – the pimps, the pickpockets, the scammers – have a definite stake in Carnaval: one of their busiest times of the year, in fact, though we might prefer not to know this.)

And each of these stakeholders has their own distinct drivers – which overlap and often conflict with those of just about everyone else…

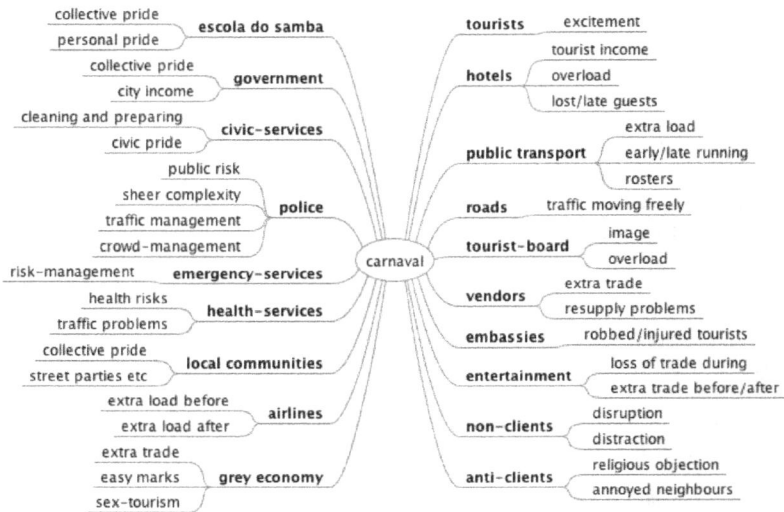

Figure 11: Carnaval – stakeholder drivers

So whose enterprise is it? Who's responsible for it? And for that matter, what *is* the 'it' that is 'the enterprise'?

To answer each of these in order, no *one* group or organisation owns the enterprise of Carnaval. If anything, it's owned by the *idea* of Carnaval itself – or perhaps more, the *feeling* of Carnaval. If anyone could be said to own it, it's probably the *escolas do samba* – the samba-schools who take part in the huge night-time parade in the Sambadromo – or the local communities who set up their vast street-parties for literally hundreds of thousands of participants at different venues all across the city.

And the question 'Who is responsible?' is a great example of how to miss the point: this is an *enterprise*, not an organisation. As we saw before, an organisation is bounded by explicit rules, roles and responsibilities; but an enterprise is bounded by vision, values and commitments – it's *emotive*, not legislative. In a sense, we're responsible to, or commit to, the shared-enterprise itself – which means that, if we choose to engage in that enterprise, we're also responsible to every other stakeholder in the enterprise, in shared commitment to the outcomes of the enterprise. And we connect with each other *through* that shared commitment: that's actually what makes the enterprise happen.

The 'it' that is 'the enterprise' is whatever is implied and bounded by an identifiable vision, values and commitments. And those in turn imply a specific *story*: the enterprise *as* story.

To make sense of that story, we might perhaps jump back to what we saw in the Dramatica model, in the earlier chapter on 'Which story?'. That model used a set of questions to identify the core components of the story's 'storymind':

- *Overall Concern*: what interests everyone in the enterprise
- *Overall Throughline*: driven by an external state, external process, internal state or internal process that affects all stakeholders
- *Overall Issue*: how the concern affects everyone in the enterprise
- *Overall Problem*: the source – apparent or actual – of what it is that affects everyone in the enterprise

In my own work with enterprises, I re-interpret this as describing the *vision* for the enterprise-story. In practice, this usually comes out in the form of a very brief 'vision-statement' – often only four or five words at most – that comprises three key components:

- the *content* or *focus* for the whole enterprise
- the *action* on that content or action
- a *qualifier* that bridges between and validates both content and action

The classic example for this is the vision for the TED conferences, as "ideas worth spreading" – 'ideas' [content], 'worth' [qualifier], 'spreading' [action]. For Carnaval we might perhaps summarise the vision as "Let's party!", but there's more to it than that: it's linked to a specific point in the year, at a specific place, and with specific values – as we'll see in a moment.

The other Dramatica questions are all worth re-exploring here, but one that probably does need extra comment is Story Limit – about whether the story is constrained more by time than, or by running out of options. In a single instance of an enterprise-story, it can be either, and for a given enterprise it will tend to be more often one than the other: but the key point is that for an enterprise to work well – especially in business terms – *the story never actually ends.*

Hence why an enterprise is more often like a series or serial: each single instance of the story has its own distinct beginning, middle and end, with its own actors and events, in accordance with the sort-of 'rules' of the enterprise's storyworld; but the storyworld itself continues on, for Next Time's Enthralling Episode. If we were ever to achieve the enterprise-vision, the story would end – and the enterprise with it. A rather important fact, that, that's killed off many an overly goal-driven organisation…

The next part here is that movement either towards or away from the 'goal' of the vision is tracked in terms of the enterprise-*values.* The most fundamental values usually end up as the 'qualifier' in the vision-statement – hence, for TED, the most important value there is that these are ideas that are *worth* spreading.

So for Carnaval, the overall idea of 'Let's party!' is tempered by some quite specific values:

- it's about *pride*, both in a personal and collective sense
- it's about *exuberance* in self-expression
- it's about *community* and *belonging*, coming together *as* a community, and in relation to and with other communities

It's not a bacchanalia, a wild drunken orgy for the sole purpose of 'getting wrecked' in a social context, as in so much binge-drinking in Britain and elsewhere. (Okay, that does happen, of course, but it actually goes against the real values of Carnaval.) Perhaps also important is that it's strongly linked to a religious context, taking place in the immediate run-up to the Christian fasting-period of Lent – in effect, a 'letting off steam' before setting down to the hard work of fasting and abstinence. So although preparation for Carnaval may well go on all year round, the festival itself does not – and probably wouldn't work if it did.

Anyway, let's look at this from the perspective of a hotel in Rio. In terms of the business-genres we explored some while back, its main enterprise is likely to be a mixed-genre somewhere between 'Road Movie' and 'You're Special'. In that sense, Carnaval is not its main focus – but it's certainly an enterprise of interest, and at the appropriate times of year, the hotel would want to align itself to that enterprise-story.

It doesn't have to *do* anything specific to align itself with that story – it's not a contract or suchlike, as it would be for organisation-to-organisation. It's just a choice, a kind of self-declaration that, for the time being, it considers itself as connected to the vision and values of the enterprise – in this case, the enterprise of Carnaval. But in doing so, some important points arise:

- aligning with the enterprise is a choice, but we do not possess that enterprise – if anything, whilst we engage in it, it possesses us...
- players whose values align most closely with the enterprise-values should take the lead
- we have our own business-values, but whilst we align with the enterprise, those values must uphold the enterprise-values as their highest priority
- by definition, every player in an enterprise is in relation with *all* other players in that enterprise – the relation may be indirect, but it always exists
- we can walk away at any time from aligning with the enterprise – but our manner of detaching from that enterprise will be viewed by all other players in terms of the values of that enterprise

One very important corollary from this is about priority of values – particularly in terms of how a business relates with a broader enterprise. Commercial businesses do need to focus on monetary profit, because otherwise they won't stay in business. But while they engage with an enterprise, the values of that enterprise *must* take priority over the business' values – *otherwise the connection with the enterprise will fail*. For example, the enterprise-values of Carnaval focus on personal pride, not monetary profit: too much of a focus on money may well be taken as an insult, both to the individual and to the collective community. Making a profit is fine, as long as the enterprise-values come first – and we'll often need to *show* how making a profit supports those broader values, too.

Another important corollary is that each enterprise has 'a cast of thousands' – or literally millions, in the case of Carnaval. Each role in effect represents a character in the enterprise-story – and in aligning with the enterprise, we do get to choose which parts we play within that story, and which parts we don't. That *is* our choice – and learning more about the nature of each enterprise will give us more scope for a more advantageous positioning in that enterprise-story, too. But *we do not 'possess' the story*: it belongs to every single one of that 'cast of thousands'. In fact if we try to 'possess' the story, we'll likely find ourselves re-cast in a different character-role to the one we'd intended – most probably as one of the 'bad-guys', in fact. Not a good idea…

The other complication is that we're rarely dealing with just one enterprise at a time: for most organisations there will be hundreds, thousands, maybe more. Each business-unit has its own enterprise, its own priorities; likewise every supplier, every customer, every employee, every profession and discipline, every quality-concern and so on. To cut down on the cacophony, it really does help to choose just one overarching enterprise – and one that is seen as 'greater than' every player in the organisation's space – so as to make clear to everyone the values by which the organisation expects to be assessed. That's '*the* enterprise' for the organisation – and it *must* be larger than the organisation itself. Which then gives us a frame for an 'outside-in' view – which in turn provides the counterpoint and counterbalance that we need for the view from 'inside-out'.

Most of the players in an enterprise are fairly easy to identify; in turn, most of those are active in their support of the enterprise and – if the organisation plays appropriately by the enterprise's 'rules' and values – in their support of the organisation's role in that enterprise. But there are three further groups who tend to be less visible, yet of whom it's often extremely important not to forget: parasites, non-clients and anti-clients.

The **parasites** of an enterprise hang around on its edges, sort-of connecting with it, but always placing their own interests above everything and everyone else. In this sense, it can be useful to think of the enterprise as a kind of ecosystem-with-purpose: and to quote Cory Doctorow, "all complex ecosystems have parasites", so the same will apply most if not all enterprises too. In the case of Carnaval, the most obvious parasites are the pimps and petty-thieves of the grey-economy; but there are, unfortunately, all too many others, including many players who purport to be essential of the enterprise itself. Whether we like it or not, parasites and more active predators do seem to be an inevitable fact of life: but it's always worth doing whatever we can to identify them and their various means of attack, and to protect the enterprise against them wherever possible.

The **non-clients** of the enterprise are affected *by* the enterprise, yet without being *in* it, or interacting with it in any direct way. For Carnaval, non-clients might include other cities, or other types of events taking place at the same time. In some cases non-clients may eventually become more engaged in the enterprise – perhaps by creating a broader scope that can include their interests – but sometimes they just want to be left alone, *and we need to respect that choice*. Above all, we need to ensure that we do not cause non-clients to become active anti-clients – because if they do, we really will be in trouble...

The **anti-clients** are *actively* engaged against the enterprise or, more usually, the organisation's engagement in that enterprise – quite often they will share the same overall vision, but strongly disagree as to how it should be achieved. For Carnaval, the anti-clients might include religious groups who object to the raucous and often overt sensuality on display, or residents of some areas who simply want to be left in peace. The key point here is that the objection is *active*, not passive: anti-clients will disrupt whatever is going on, wherever they can, and in whatever way they can – and often show good reason for doing so, too. For the organisation, the only way out is to re-engage them in the enterprise, and ensure that their voice is acknowledged and respected – otherwise a lot of damage can be caused to the organisation and its aims, often without apparent warning.

Anyway, enough on that for now – we'll no doubt come back to it again later.

Application

- An organisation-centric 'inside-out' view, or an enterprise-oriented 'outside-in' view: which seems more natural to you? Which would seem more natural to others in your organisation? In each case, why is this so?
- Comparing 'inside-out' and 'outside-in', what does each view highlight? What does each view tend to hide or ignore? How do you achieve a balance between these views, to gain a better sense of the whole?
- Which enterprises does your organisation connect with, in order to achieve its own vision and aims? Which is the main story – the core shared-enterprise – that links all of those stories together?

- What are the vision and values for each of the enterprise-stories with which your organisation connects? What are the mutual commitments that hold each enterprise together? In what ways is each player assessed in terms of how well it upholds the values of the enterprise?
- How do you balance between all the different enterprises with which your organisation will engage? Within the architecture, how do you balance all the conflicting priorities of values? How do you demonstrate alignment with and support of each of the different sets of values?
- What is the overarching 'the enterprise' for your organisation? In what ways can you ensure that every aspect of the organisation's architecture will link to and support that enterprise? Architecturally, how can you ensure that all metrics and measures align with that enterprise's values?
- Who or what are the parasites of each enterprise? What damage can they cause, to the enterprise, and to your organisation's engagement in the enterprise? What can you do to minimise or prevent their predations?
- Who are the relevant non-clients or anti-clients of the enterprise, or of your organisation's engagement in the enterprise? What impacts can or do they have on the enterprise or on your organisation? What can you do to reduce the risks? What, architecturally, can you do to prevent non-clients from becoming active anti-clients? What can you do to engage with the anti-clients, and regain their respect?

INTERLUDE

What's the story? How does an enterprise-story actually *work*? In search of ideas from other domains, I turn to the games-designer Chris Crawford's book *Chris Crawford on Interactive Storytelling*, and the insights just flow:

- "stories are about *people*" – downplay any focus on 'things', because they're just props to help the people-story along

Going back to those earlier distinctions, the organisation seems to be mostly about *things*, including people-as-things; the enterprise seems more about *people*, perhaps including things-as-people?

- "stories are not puzzles to be 'solved'" – a puzzle may play a key part, but it's still a *people*-story

Again on organisation versus enterprise, it seems the organisation is focussed primarily on puzzles, on simplistic single-answer sort-of-stories with a predefined process and predefined outcome; but the enterprise allows – or more, encourages – the *un*expected, the different, the new.

- "story*world* not story*line*" – it's about possibilities, not predestined paths

Same again: that organisation-centric 'inside-out' view prefers to push people onto the predefined storyline of processes – but it's that quote by Chris Potts again, that "customers do not appear in our processes, we appear in their experiences". Very different.

- "spectacle does not make stories" – spectacle is not *in itself* a story

The same would be true for the 'spectacle' of product-features and the like, I guess? And the dreaded 'marketing razzmatazz', too…

- "stories need a conflict of some form" – but that's not the same as violence

Violence isn't conflict, it's a *context* for conflict – 'spectacle' again, with no inherent connection to story. As Crawford puts it, "stories are about the exercise of emotion, not musculature". Violence-based metaphors such as 'business is war' have been way over-used, and they mostly don't make sense in practice anyway. For the enterprise, we're going to need different ideas about 'conflict': focus more on the tensions beneath the surface conflict, perhaps?

- "stories are about *choices* that the characters must make" – likewise the human consequences for each of those choices

An important point there about *time* – that within enterprise-as-system and enterprise-as-story, those 'consequences' may well not always follow a simple linear cause-effect logic.

- "stories take place on stages, not maps" – a big difference about being *in* the story, versus abstract overview *of* the story

Back to the 'where' of story: another variant of that old theme that 'the map is not the territory', perhaps. Important for enterprise-architecture, anyway – and also possible dangers for management being dependent on abstract metrics rather than live experience.

- "participation is not necessarily interaction" – passive 'consumer' versus active *engagement* in the story

A movie is one-sided participation ('do it *to* me'); a real enterprise-type story is a two-way interaction ('do it *with* me'). No guesses as to which of those the classic command-and-control model would prefer – but the result isn't a *story*.

- "interactivity [is] a *cyclic* process between two or more *active* agents in which each agent alternately listens, thinks and speaks" – and *acts*, too

It's like that earlier description of narrative: 'something happens; and then something else happens' – a *cycle*. But not necessarily a simple repetition – that whole theme of 'and something *unexpected* happened'. And not necessarily just a simple alternation, either: not as per those often overly-simplistic protocol-diagrams we see in so many BPMN models. There's more to it than that…

- "you must have good listening *and* good thinking *and* good speaking to have good interaction" – it's not just one or the other, we need all of them, in balance, to make the story work

In terms of business-process, listening is acceptance of the input; 'thinking' is the internals of that process; and 'speaking' is the output. Again, though, the key is the *story* – not just the process.

And one last, very interesting note from the book:

- "in tragedy, the reward is applause, not victory" – true to the vision and values of the enterprise, also placing collective above self

Might well apply to areas such as customer-service: would explain the well-known point that people are often *more* happy even when we haven't managed to fix a problem, as long as we've honest about what went wrong. Hmm…

Anyway, enough reading for now. Looking for a more direct way to make sense of story, I drop in on a meetup of the local creative-writing group: an evening of exercises, experimenting with story-form in various ways.

We talk about 'voice', the ways we make each character different and distinctive on the written page. Reminds me of the *Cluetrain Manifesto*:

> Conversations among human beings *sound* human. They are conducted in a human voice.
>
> Whether delivering information, opinions, perspectives, dissenting arguments or humorous asides, the human voice is typically open, natural, uncontrived. People recognize each other as such from the sound of this voice.
>
> Most corporations, on the other hand, only know how to talk in the soothing, humorless monotone of the mission statement, marketing brochure, and your-call-is-important-to-us busy signal. Same old tone, same old lies.

One of the writing-group is a young German lass, her clear English accented less by her native country than by a strong Irish brogue. "I spent nine months studying in Galway", she says, "the dialect was too easy to pick up!" Interesting how some places so strongly invite us to become part of their story, whilst others seem to slide past without ever engaging our attention. Odd… Might be something useful there about 'stage' versus 'story', perhaps: yet another idea to explore.

Better get back to the story, though.

Application

- What other domains can you turn to for new ideas about your own organisation's industry and enterprise? What insights do you gain from this? How *do* you 'make the connection', linking and 'translating' between the different domains to find something new that's of practical use in your work?
- Looking at those quotes from Chris Crawford above, what insights do you gain about your own organisation and enterprise? How would you apply those insights in practice?

- What is your own organisation's 'voice'? Does it seem "open, natural, uncontrived"? Or is it just "the humorless monotone of the mission-statement"? If the latter, what might be done, in *architectural* terms, to bring it to be less robotic, more human?
- Does your organisation, or each part of the organisation, have its own distinct accent or dialect? How quickly do people pick up that accent? In what ways does that accent impact on what they say, or how they say it? What effect does it have on how people relate to the enterprise story? If need be, what *architectural* choices do you have to change this?

12: FINDING THE VOICE

What's the story? Well, it's always about *people*: that part seems clear enough by now. And if it's about people, it's also about the *voice* of each of those people: not just 'the story', but many, many stories, many voices, all interweaving with each other.

The catch, then, is to prevent it collapsing into cacophony…

Perhaps best to start from the voice itself. Who *are* each of these people? They're all individuals, each with their own story: not a statistic, not a 'persona', but a person in their own right. What *is* their voice?

We might hear about 'the voice of the Customer', but what about 'voice of the Employee' too? – that 'cast of thousands' again, the active drivers of the organisation's relationship with the enterprise and its story. Much of *their* voice comes through in action – and it's important to acknowledge that voice *as* action.

For example, notice how film-credits have changed over the years: who and what gets acknowledged, and where and when in the film. For decades, only a few 'key players' would be headlined at the start – the director, producer, the lead actors, perhaps the cinematographer and casting-director – with nothing at the end but 'The End'. That list at the front gets longer for a while, and then suddenly we start to get end-credits - which get longer, and longer, and longer. Thirty years ago it would have been just the cast-list and the senior film-crew; but now? Page after page of them: software-designers, database-administrators, assistants to assistants, even the accountants. And, often, families and babies too: look at the end-credits of any Pixar film. In short, it's not just the 'heroes' of the film-making world: it's everyone, everyday people, with everyday lives. A much more *human* story behind the story of the film itself.

What's sad is how very few other industries do the same kinds of acknowledgement of their employees' hard work…

Another point here is simply about how to *listen*. For example, Shawn Callahan and colleagues at strategy-consultancy Anecdote developed a set of techniques for what they term *story-listening*:

Story-listening is the process of eliciting and collecting stories, helping groups to draw meaning from those stories, and then, most importantly from a business perspective, creating opportunities for the stories to inspire employees to take positive, transformational action. … It is all about helping those who can most influence change understand what's really happening in their organisation, and then inspiring them to do something about it. All good business story-work is purposeful.

Story-listening is all about listening out for the voice, for the ways in which people engage and express themselves within the overall shared-enterprise. Shawn Callahan again:

All the stories you hear at work reflect your organisation's culture. You cannot change this culture without changing the stories being told and retold in your workplace. Then, once you've initiated new behaviours, new stories will flow. Story-listening helps you become aware of the current corporate narratives – it helps you to clearly hear the dominant stories, the prevalent archetypes, the repeating plot lines. Most importantly, because you are working with stories, your feelings are engaged, and these feelings inspire you to take action. Story-listening gives you the essential ingredients for change: decisions makers who both understand what's going on *and* who are emotionally moved to make a difference.

And if no-one's listening at all to those voices, what we'd have is the risks implied in the *Cluetrain Manifesto*:

People in networked markets have figured out that they get far better information and support from one another than from vendors. So much for corporate rhetoric about adding value to commoditized products.

There are no secrets. The networked market knows more than companies do about their own products. And whether the news is good or bad, they tell everyone.

What's happening to markets is also happening among employees. A metaphysical construct called 'The Company' is the only thing standing between the two.

Don't forget that this isn't just about story: it's about story within architecture – architecture *as* story, story *as* architecture. Feelings and engagement are what drive the enterprise: people engage in the enterprise when they feel that their voice – in whatever form – is heard. No voice, no action – or no engagement, anyway.

In that sense, storylistening is a key component of the architecture – if 'component' is the right word here. It's not just that we use storylistening and the like within our work: we need to embed it within the structures, too. *Supporting the conversation is part of the architecture.*

This is still alien territory for many organisations – especially for those that still believe that they possess the story. The old model of command-and-control assumes there's no conversation at all – just 'orders from the top', to be obeyed at once, without question. A nice self-satisfying myth for some, perhaps, but in reality it's never worked all that well, especially in contexts of rapid change. And that kind of change *is* coming through, whether anyone likes it or not. To quote *Cluetrain* again:

> There are two conversations going on. One inside the company. One with the market.

> These two conversations want to talk to each other. They are speaking the same language. They recognize each other's voices.

> Smart companies will get out of the way and help the inevitable to happen sooner.

I don't think it's quite as simple as "get out of the way": there *is* still a real need to keep track of the story, and to give it some kind of direction. That matters; and it's an *architectural* matter as well. But we do need to rethink it in terms of the broader story – the story of the *enterprise*, not just of the organisation.

And that broader story is always about *people*. To use that classic cliché from Shakespeare's *As You Like It*:

> All the world's a stage,
> And all the men and women merely players;
> They have their exits and their entrances,
> And one man in his time plays many parts...

So each enterprise is a story; and each player – each stakeholder in the enterprise-story – has a role that they *choose* within that story. Some of those players are the actors, visible on the stage; some are stage-crew, behind the scenes; others are front-of-house, meeting-and-greeting at the door; some are the audience, participating in a less active sense, perhaps, but still very much engaged in the story. And there's the management, too, of the theatre, and of the story – the director, the producer, the choreographer and suchlike.

All with different roles in the story-of-the-story. And each with their own distinctive voice, striving to be heard.

We could usefully extend that analogy to include casting – find the right place for each voice within the overall story. There's a very good reason why the casting-director gets priority placing in the film-credits: casting is one of the most crucial factors that can make or break the execution of a story. Why is why, as architects, we *do* need to include a strong understanding of HR and the like throughout our architectures…

If the company tries to possess the story, it's like a stage-play with a prompter standing in the wings, yelling out everyone's lines and preventing the *emergence* of the story: pretty soon all of the actors – and everyone else, for that matter – will give up in disgust and walk away. And, more to the point, move off to share their voice in a different play, a different shared-enterprise – one that doesn't involve this organisation.

To paraphrase Chris Potts:

> Customers do not appear in our processes –
> we appear in their *stories*.

We need to remember that customers – and employees too – can take their stories away at any time. And the whole point here is that we do want them to link their story to ours. Our organisation acts within the scope of the overall enterprise: so we *always* need to think broader-enterprise first – outside-in, not inside-out. And we also need to ensure that each voice is heard – without losing track of the story.

As an organisation, what we *need* is engagement in our chosen enterprise-story. And emotion is always key to that engagement. All professional storytellers understand this point – particularly the creators of the 'imaginary worlds' of television sci-fi. People engage intensely within those stories: the term 'fan' is shorthand for 'fanatic', and it shows. That intense shared commitment to the shared-enterprise of the story is part of what keeps the story going; and more to the point, without that commitment, the story fades and is forgotten. The exact same applies to the story for a business-enterprise: without the same shared-commitment to the enterprise-story, the business fades and is forgotten. Which is why this is important…

The show's fans will, in an almost literal sense, place themselves in those imaginary worlds, imagine themselves or their characters in that invented space. Marketers aim to do the same, by likewise creating a story – a strategy of which Apple, for example, is one of the great masters. The structures of the architecture provide the stage for that story; yet the architecture also *is* the story, extending *beyond* the organisation itself, allowing all the players to *be* their chosen roles within that wider story.

The challenge is to ensure that the story allows all of this openness yet still retains its integrity. The storytellers do this by viewing themselves not as 'possessors' of the story, but as its *custodians*: the difference is subtle, but extremely important – not 'control', but *trust*.

They also acknowledge that much of 'their' story will extend far beyond their own organisation, across many different channels, many different media – social-media, fan websites, or whatever. Some of those side-connections never touch the organisation at all – and yet they all matter to the story. It's been interesting to watch the development of a trend towards 'transmedia storytelling', in which different parts of a story will appear on different media, linked together only by chasing the threads of story across all of those different spaces. In that way, the organisation can extend the reach of its own distinct voice and story, engaging with the other voices and stories in that shared enterprise-story – and without attempting to drown out all other voices in a futile attempt at 'control' the story.

Anyway, back to *Cluetrain* once more for a final word on this, and perhaps a final warning:

> To speak with a human voice, companies must share the concerns of their communities.
>
> But first, they must belong to a community.
>
> Companies must ask themselves where their corporate cultures end.
>
> If their cultures end before the community begins, they will have no market.
>
> Human communities are based on discourse – on human speech about human concerns.
>
> The community of discourse is the market.
>
> Companies that do not belong to a community of discourse will die.

Suggests there's some real challenges for our architectures there: and some real tensions, too.

Application

- If your organisation was a film, who would be listed in the film-credits? Where would their names be placed within those credits, and why? What would that positioning tell you, and others, the perceived importance of each person to the overall enterprise? And who would it be that gets to choose the positioning of those names?

- For many films, the credits often include many people beyond the boundaries of the organisation itself – sometimes even the families and children of employees, as in those Pixar films. If your organisation was a film, where would that boundary of acknowledgement be placed? Why? And by whom?

- Perhaps just as important, whose names and roles would *not* be included within those credits? Whose voice is *not* acknowledged? Why not? And who gets to choose who's in, and who's out?

- Does your organisation encourage any employees to 'sign' their work in some way? If so, what forms does that 'signing' take? What difference does it make to employees' morale? Or to customers' engagement with the organisation?

- What story-listening and other narrative-based work do you do within your enterprise-architecture practice? If any, is this only within the organisation, or beyond the organisation as well? With whom do you share and develop the insights that arise from this work? And if you don't do any narrative-work yourselves, does any else in the organisation do so? If not, why not?

- If no-one in your architecture-practice, or even in your organisation, is doing narrative-enquiry with customers and employees, what Cluetrain-type risks arise for the organisation as a whole? What impact and implications would these risks have for the organisation's architectures?

- What *are* the conversations within the enterprise? Whose are the voices? In an architecture that's often so filled with machines, how do we retain that human voice?

- Within your organisation, who perhaps tries to *possess* the story? What architectural options do you have to encourage them to loosen their grip, to pull back to more a role of 'custodian' than 'controller' of the story? What structures and stories can you use to help them more to *trust* others' voices and choices in this?

- Who or what manages the casting of roles within the overall story? In terms of organisation, what *are* the rules and responsibilities associated with each role? In terms of enterprise, what are the vision, values and mutual commitments that hold the story together? What part does the architecture play in supporting these sides of the story?

- What is it that engages other people in the enterprise-story? And what is it that might drive them away from that story? What happens to your perception of this once you choose to view the story as an *architectural* issue, and hence an explicit part of your professional responsibility?

- Through what channels is the story told? What parts of the story are told through each channel? If 'the medium is the message', in what ways does the medium itself change the voice through which that part of the story can be told?

- "Human communities are based on discourse, on human speech about human concerns" – within the architecture, how do you ensure that this 'human speech on human concerns' is heard? And by whom? For what purpose, and what action?

13: MAINTAIN THE TENSION

In a conventional Hollywood-style story, the key driver is some form of conflict. But in a business-context, conflict is usually what we'd most want to avoid... So instead, the key story-driver is the tension between what is desired, versus what actually exists in the present – the tension between reality and the enterprise-vision.

Let's describe this in visual form. Start off with a single thread of tension, from where we are now to some desired end. It may be achievable – a goal – or never actually achievable – as is typical for an enterprise-vision – but there's actually no difference for this kind of abstraction: it's just a tension, a driver, a desire.

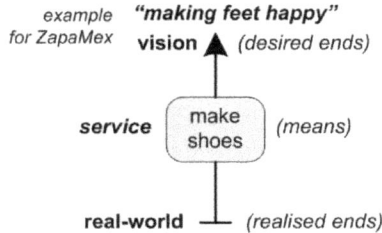

Figure 12: Tension from realised-ends to vision

As soon as there's conflict, an unrequited tension, straight away we have the makings of a story: "how do we get from here to there?", "what are the challenges that we face?", and so on. And as soon as there's more than one person with the same desire or aim, straight away we have a *shared* story – and hence potential for a shared enterprise.

Figure 13: Tension to shared-vision

78

It's the same overall story, but different players will have different capabilities, yet also different needs. And because they share the same overall aim, they have common ground with each other: so they *assist each other* in finding their respective ways towards the shared aim. That's the 'offer', the 'value-proposition': it's a way of helping another player within the same enterprise reach towards their vision. Value is created as these offers move around the shared-enterprise; and that value in turn is measured in terms of the set of values that are implied by the vision. Or, alternatively, we could say that shared-value is measured in terms of how much it eases the tension between the 'now' and the desired-future.

Yes, I know, very technical, very abstract, not much like a story. But that's *actually* what happens in a successful marketing-effort: as Hagel, Brown and Davison explain in their book *The Power of Pull*, we don't 'push' products or services at people, we create a 'pull' that brings other players in the enterprise towards us. And we create that pull, and the relationship that underpins it, *because* we demonstrate that we share the same vision, the same story, the same tension.

The usual organisation-centric view of our relationships with the market would look like this:

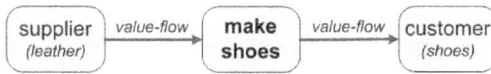

Figure 14: Simple supply-chain relationships

But an enterprise-oriented view of those relationships would be a value-web, more like this:

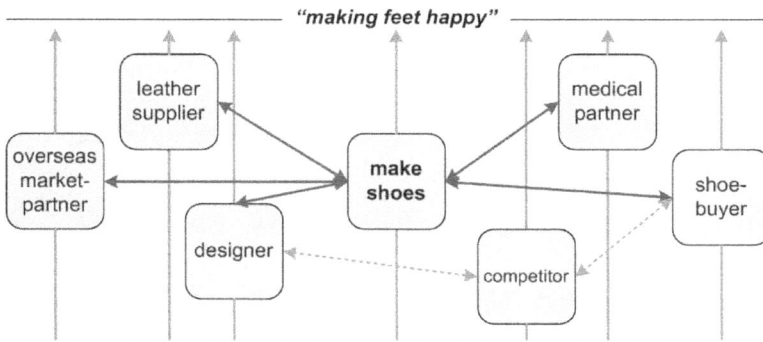

Figure 15: Value-web relationships

Which brings us back to Chris Potts' quote again: that it's not that customers – or anyone else – would appear in our processes, but that *we* appear in their experiences. Just as they appear as players within our story, we appear as players in their stories. And for the time and *at* the time that the interaction takes place, it's the *same* story: within that variously-brief moment, the stories align. That's how this all works.

For much the same reasons, structure alone is not enough. "Build it and they will come" is a nice idea, but if the tension isn't there, they won't come, no matter how much we work on that structure. What brings them there is the tension – the *story*.

Which would also tell us that an architecture that's focussed only on structure will never be enough: it's only by bringing structure together with story that we can make sense of what's actually needed in the enterprise, and in our organisation's role within that enterprise.

This also brings us back to those core questions:

- what does it mean?
- what's the point?
- where do *I* fit in this story?
- what's in it for me?

Each of those questions indicates a kind of tension, a literal quest – so if we want to engage people in the enterprise-story, we need to show how that story also links to and mitigates the tension of their quest. Each answer – what it means, its point, where they fit, and its value to them – reduces that tension, yet *also* engages them in the broader tension of the enterprise-vision and its story.

We see much the same with improvisation and real-time response, or with Agile-style development and the like. The time-pressures and the inherent-uncertainties provide their own tension, but the connection to the tension of the shared enterprise-story actually *reduces* the tension of the uncertainty: the vision acts as a compass, imparts direction; the values provide a means against which to monitor success or failure. It's all in the story – and in the *tension* of the story.

So where *is* this story? We *know* where the story is: it's in process-volume, in capability-development, business-scenario, strategy or use-case, resource-management; in every standard, protocol and transaction; it's in governance, in opportunities, in risks; and it's certainly in every customer-experience, every customer-journey.

Once we know where and how to look, story is *everywhere* in our enterprise-architecture. And everywhere there's story, there's also tension – because that tension is *why* it's a story.

That tension is the *driver* for the story: it's the 'why' that's behind whatever happens within that story. In business, we'd most often see this as a *process*: each traverse through a business-process is a self-contained story with its own actors, actions and events.

From the organisation's perspective, process is about the use of structure; but from an enterprise perspective, we see that process more as part of *plot*, the unfolding of story. Note, though, that it's not necessarily a simple linear unwinding of tension: for example, as we saw earlier, the tensions of a sales-process might well follow the up-and-down roller-coaster of the Hero's Journey pattern. Plot can be more than a bit tangled at times… – especially at the larger scale.

There's also the tension of the overall story within each stage of the Story-Cycle – and *between* each stage in that cycle, too, within every possible scope and scale. That tension is what drives the story-cycle onward from one stage to the next:

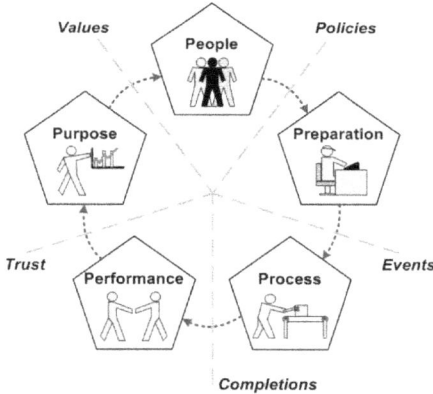

Figure 16: Story-cycle

The same applies in the Strategy-Cycle. The story always starts in emotion, in feeling, but that same tension pulls it forward into the thinking-work of preparation and planning, and then into action. From there, the tensions between those different modes unwind again, first to the more thinking-oriented modes of reflection, and finally the connection back to the initial intent, the original story:

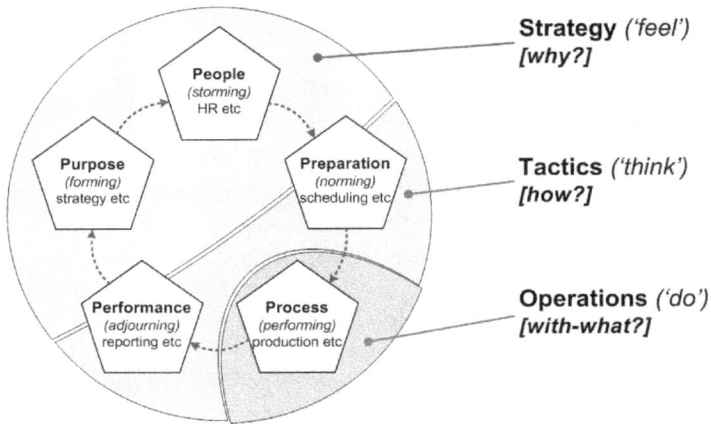

Figure 17: Strategy-cycle

Then there are the tensions and transitions of the Market-Cycle:

- everything starts from **trust** (or *reputation*, which is a kind of second-hand trust)
- once there is trust, it's possible to build mutual-**respect** and relationship
- given the relationship, it's then possible to gain **attention** for an offer
- with acceptance of the offer, the **transaction** follows
- after the transaction there's an explicit **completion**, to reaffirm the trust and connect back to the original intent

In this sense, everything in the market-story begins and ends with trust. To put this in more visual form:

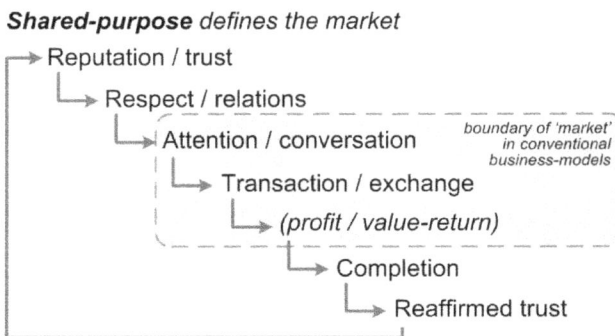

Figure 18: Market-cycle

There are some variations on this – they're not so much stages as *dimensions* – but the connections do tend to follow a virtuous-cycle of this form.

And if we map the Market-Cycle onto the Story-Cycle, we have a story-structure that shows how a sales-process and suchlike needs to work, and the tensions that pull it onward from one stage to the next:

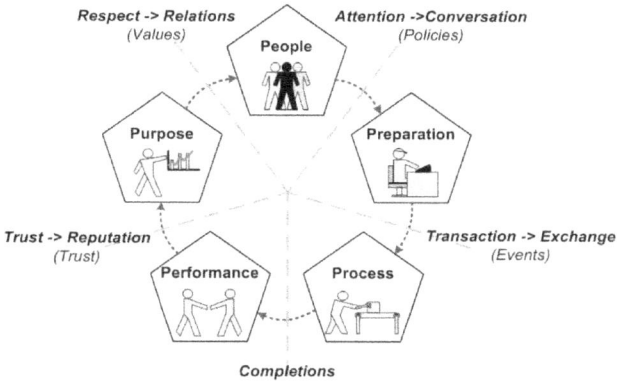

Figure 19: Story-cycle and Market-cycle

In all these cases we *want* that tension to exist – otherwise there's no drive, and no story.

So maintain the tension – because the tension *is* the story.

Yet avoid conflict – because *no-one* wins from conflict.

An interesting balancing-act…

Application

- What conflicts do you see across the enterprise, across your organisation, within the architecture for your organisation? What impacts do they have? What can you do within your architecture to mitigate those conflicts, and reduce their risks?
- Across all of those spaces, what are the tensions that *don't* collapse into conflict? In what ways do those tensions drive the story forward?
- What difference does it make to shift the perspective from 'push' to 'pull'? In what ways do those differences in perspective demand different architectures to support them? What would you need to change within your architecture to

support a transition from 'push' to 'pull', from inside-out to outside-in?

- What difference does it make to view the relationships with the market not as a simple throughline supply-chain, but as a more interactive value-web? How could you use architecture to support a different role within those relationships? What would you need to change within your architecture to support this change of story?

- "Build it and they will come" – where do you see examples of this error within your organisation and its architecture? Given the connection between structure and story, what story can you create that would give that structure a stronger reason to exist? What metrics would you need in order to demonstrate return-on-reclaimed-investment from this re-thinking of the story?

- What happens to your view of the architecture if you shift the perspective from process to plot? What are the plot-lines, the plot-points, in that story? Who are the players at each point in the plot? How does the tension at each point in the plot serve to drive the story forward?

- Feeling, thinking doing: which of these modes are given more priority within your architecture, and why? What can do you to bring them into better balance? How can you use the tensions between these modes to drive the story as a virtuous-cycle?

- "Everything in the market-story begins and ends with trust" – where is trust included within your architecture, as a driver for the story? In what ways does your architecture ensure that explicit connection with trust – especially in each entity's relationships with the broader enterprise? In what ways would your architecture need to change, to give stronger support for the Market-Cycle?

- "Maintain the tension, but avoid conflict" – how would you best do this within the architecture?

INTERLUDE

Yet another distraction, it seems: once again I'm probably at risk of getting too tied up in the technical side of story. Oh well.

Anyway, what's going on right now is that I'm delving deeper into the Dramatica view of story, and in particular its ideas about character. It talks about distinctions between main-character and impact-character:

- *main-character* provides our point of view into the story
- *impact-character* blocks the way, provides the contrast

The tensions between these two characters – or entities, to be more pedantic – provide the energy that drives the story.

Dramatica then contrasts 'main' and 'impact' with the more usual Hollywood-type ideas about protagonist and antagonist. Within the classic Hollywood story, protagonist and main-character are merged into the same person, 'the hero'. And antagonist and impact-character are likewise merged into the same person or entity – typically portrayed as 'the villain'.

But that fixed pattern tends to give us very clichéd, stereotypic stories. What Dramatica explains is that the main-character is not always the protagonist, and the impact-character is not necessarily the antagonist: they're different story-functions.

Overall, Dramatica describes eight distinct archetypic story-roles:

protagonist is the driver of the story, the one around whom the action revolves

antagonist is directly opposed to the protagonist, and represents the challenge that must be overcome for the protagonist's story to succeed

reason makes its decisions and takes action on the basis of logic, never letting feelings get in the way of a rational course

emotion responds with its feelings without thinking, whether it is angry or kind, with disregard for practicality

skeptic doubts everything – courses of action, sincerity, truth, whatever

sidekick is unfailing in its loyalty and support, often of the protagonist, though may be attached to the antagonist instead

guardian is a teacher or helper who aids in the quest and offers a moral standard

contagonist has its own agenda, and may hinder, delude and tempt the protagonist to take the wrong course or approach

The main-character and impact-character can take on any of these archetype-roles; and likewise for other characters in the story. In fact there's a many-to-many relationship between character and story-role: a single character may take on more than one story-role, and a story-role may be shared between multiple characters.

How we would view these archetype-roles, and to whom or what we might assign them, will be different according to how we view the story. From the organisation's inside-out view, for example, a competitor might be considered an antagonist, directly opposed to the organisation's success. But if we take an enterprise-oriented outside-in view of the story – though still with the organisation as main-character – then a competitor is just a contagonist: it's not "a challenge that must be overcome", but more that it "has its own agenda", trying to pull the story into its own preferred direction. Implies a different relationship. Interesting.

More structure-stuff. Just hope it's some use in *this* story, that's all.

Application

- Everyone would, we hope, be the main-character of their own story, and the same should apply to organisations too – but if so, who or what is the impact-character of that story? From which perspective?

- In what ways does the relationship between the impact-character and the organisation-as-main-character create the tension that drives the story?

- Who or what takes on the archetypic roles of protagonist and antagonist within the organisation's inside-out view of the story? And in the broader-enterprise's outside-in view of the same story? In what ways do these differ? How? And why?

- Those other Dramatica archetype-roles of reason, emotion, skeptic, sidekick, guardian, contagonist – who would these be, from the organisation's perspective? And from the broader outside-in perspective of the enterprise? In what ways do these role-assignments differ in each view? How? And why?

14: BETRAYING THE STORY

The good-guys, and the bad-guys: you'll see them in almost every Hollywood movie. It's always easy to see who the good-guys are: they're the protagonists of the story. (Strangely, that's still true even if the good-guys are actually bad-guys by any other standard – they're the 'good-guys' *from the story's point of view*.) But if so, who are the bad-guys? Where do the bad-guys come from? And why *are* they the bad-guys, anyway?

Businesses aren't Hollywood – most of them, anyway. But those Hollywood-style notions of 'good-guys' (us, of course) and 'bad-guys' (them – or someone we can describe as 'them') are perhaps almost as prevalent. The catch is that, in practice, those ideas are way too simplistic, and cause way too much unhelpful conflict: we need a better way of looking at this.

For example, if we're the good-guys, does that make everyone else the bad-guys? It might sometimes seem like that when things go wrong, but it's perhaps not the wisest of moves to start off by assuming that every supplier and customer is a bad-guy: doesn't help for building trust in the market-cycle, anyway…

Using some types of models can get even crazier than that, as an enterprise-architect in a military context explained:

> We were trying to use a supply-chain frame to model all of the Army's inter-entity relationships – but we realised it wouldn't work when the only way it would let us describe the Enemy was as a customer!

To make sense of this in a way that works, we need to rethink the structure of the story, using some of the themes we've come across so far in this story:

- the story we're working with is always the *human* story of the enterprise
- the organisation is only one player within a much larger enterprise-story
- there are many sub-stories within that main story – some of which may not touch the organisation, but by definition will affect it in some way because it's *in* the same overall story

- every sub-story takes place within the storyworld of the enterprise, and is subject to the values of that enterprise and the implied 'rules' of its genre
- each sub-story has its beginning, middle and end, but the story of the overall enterprise is more likely to be a never-quite-ending series or serial than a single-shot
- every sub-story, and the story as a whole, is driven by the tension between what currently exists and what is desired – the aim of every enterprise is to resolve that tension
- although ultimately each sub-story of the enterprise is rooted in a *human* endeavour, each nominal player in that sub-story may be individual or collective, and any combination of human, machine, IT-system or something else entirely
- each sub-story may have 'a cast of thousands', but we view it at each moment from the perspective of a single main-character – which may be any type of player, human or otherwise
- the story is propelled forward by the relationship between the main-character and an 'impact-character' – someone or something that at that moment represents the tension of the enterprise-story
- all of these story-roles move around from player to player – ultimately it's the story of the enterprise, not of any individual player
- our architecture exists to provide structures that support these stories of the enterprise – "a vehicle for the telling of stories, a canvas for relaying societal myths, a stage for the theater of everyday life"

Okay, I know it's yet another very structural view of story, but to put it into more human terms:

- the main-character provides our point of view into the story
- the impact-character blocks the way, and presents the contrast and the tension that are the *reason* to act or change within the realm and rules of the storyworld

Although it's a lot easier to describe the story from the perspective of a single character, it often makes more sense to keep it moving from character to character, to build a more rounded view of the whole. Kind of like the story of the blind men and the elephant, really.

The main character is not always the protagonist – it can be any of those Dramatica archetypes, or any combination of them. And the impact-character is not necessarily the 'bad-guy' – though it will often feel like that from the main-character's perspective, precisely because it's forcing the main-character into a change or action that it probably doesn't *want* to do, but *needs* to do in order to resolve the tensions of the story.

So, given all of that, who *are* the bad-guys?

Short answer: *the bad-guys are anyone or anything that acts against the aims of the shared-enterprise.*

But notice that it's about the aims of the *enterprise* – not necessarily the aims of the *organisation*. This is an absolutely crucial point that too many people still seem to miss – and one that can become extremely important wherever the organisation's aims don't quite align with those of the enterprise.

So from an *enterprise* perspective, would the competitors of our organisation be classed as the bad-guys? Not really: no more than for our own organisation, in fact. Even to our organisation they're best described as contagonists – "has its own agenda, and may hinder, delude and tempt the protagonist to take the wrong course or approach".

What about the parasites of the enterprise, such as the pickpockets and pimps at Carnaval – are they the bad-guys? Again, not really: in most cases they're little more than a nuisance, a distraction from the story – the 'giggle-wreckers', to use Peter O'Donnell's lovely term.

What about the non-clients, at the extremities of the enterprise? No, they're like extras on a film-set – they may not play an active part in the story, but it wouldn't be the same story without them.

Then what about our anti-clients? – because they're definitely the bad-guys as far as *our* organisation is concerned... Maybe so: but from the enterprise perspective, our anti-clients are often some of our most important *allies*, because their actions 'against' us serve to remind us about what the enterprise-story really is – as opposed to whatever self-centred delusion that the organisation might be following at present...

Where do anti-clients come from? In some cases they'll be all but inherent in the enterprise: for example, if we're providing family-planning services, we'll be up against religious objections; if we drill for oil in the Antarctic, we'll be up against environmentalists and the like. And in terms of the narrative-paradigm, their view of the enterprise-story *will* have its own 'good reasons' – so at the least, we do need to be respectful there.

Even more, once we understand that we *are* in the same story, we can recognise them *as* allies, rather than as 'enemies'. Look at the Market-Cycle again: by building trust, we create space for respect and relationship; from there, we have a basis for conversation; and thence for mutually-beneficial transactions of one kind or another. Walmart did this: after decades of dismissing every critique from environmentalists and other activists, they turned it round, and asked them for help in lifting their own game. And did, in ways by which everyone wins: improved sustainability *and* lower costs, in every sense of 'cost'.

Likewise, in that Army context, the Enemy is often actually a kind of anti-client – someone who *does* share a commitment to the same overall enterprise-story, but (very!) strongly disagrees about how to achieve it. I remember reading a US Army publication a few years back that described something very similar to the Walmart story: huge success in ending a long guerrilla war, not by military force, but by shifting their *own* view of the Enemy, first to that of anti-clients, and then as allies in the same shared-enterprise.

So how *does* someone become a 'bad-guy' for the enterprise? The answer is that it's the same way that an organisation creates its own anti-clients: *by betraying the enterprise-story.*

Take a look at the most hated organisations: as you'll see from any Twitter-search with a #fail hashtag, it's usually the telcos and other utility-service corporations that top the list in most every country, followed closely by airlines and parcel-services. Why? It's because they make promises that they either can't or won't keep.

In other words, *they're betraying the story* of the enterprise to which they say they've aligned. Almost by definition, any player who betrays the story – acts against the values of the enterprise-story – is instantly a 'bad-guy' to every other player in that enterprise. Not a good idea...

There are two common ways in which organisations betray the story. One is by becoming so self-centred, so stuck in 'inside-out' thinking, that they forget even that they're *in* a shared-enterprise. For example, they think of their customers not as partners in a joint endeavour, but as passive 'subjects' who, as one friend put it, have no other function than to "consume products and crap cash". For enterprise-architects, creating an enterprise-oriented 'outside-in' view is often an essential corrective for this kind of commercial suicide...

The other way of betraying the story – usually a somewhat slower and more subtle form of shared suicide – is endemic wherever the money-men are allowed to dominate the organisation's own story. It's actually caused by a failure to understand the immutability of the Story-Cycle, and the reason is that there are *three* distinct types of completion in the transition-phase immediately after a Process or transaction ends. All three of these completions aim to continue the story-cycle; but the first two completions also allow an option to take a short-cut, back to an earlier part of the cycle – and that's where the problems arise. We see this best in a mapping onto the Market-Cycle:

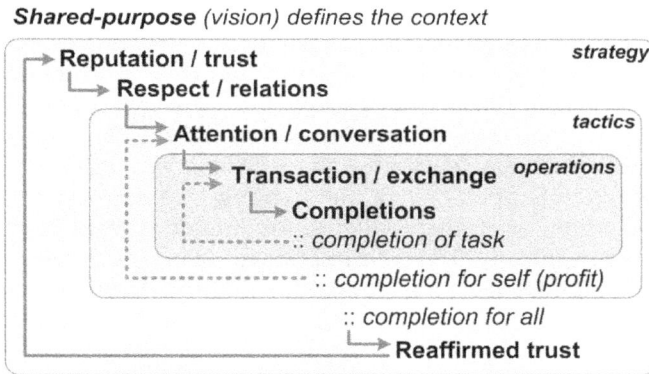

Figure 20: Market-cycle – three completions

The first step is *completion of process*. As soon as that's done, we can continue on, or jump back to the start of the same Process, to keep production-speed as high as possible. And that's okay, as long as we don't get stuck in that short-cut loop: because if we do, we'll end up in the classic Communist-style mistake of churning out vast quantities of out-of-date product with no market – and quite soon no business, either.

The second step is *completion for Self* – which, in a business context, is actually the point at which monetisation occurs. As soon as that finishes, we again have a choice to continue on, or take a short-cut back to the start of the next business-transaction. Which is what we'd probably *want* to do, because it's the way to maximise profit in the *short*-term. Yet notice the catch: we can take that short-cut *some* of the time, but not *all* the time – because if we do, the *long-term* result is always lethal for the organisation...

The third step is *completion for Enterprise* – completion both for the customer, and from the perspective of other 'interested parties' further out within the shared-enterprise. In terms of story, we'd see this in the completion of a customer-journey somewhere *beyond* the organisation; we'd see it as a story of customer-satisfaction; or we'd see it some city-official expressing pride at the presence of the organisation in their city. We'd also see it in the way that both story-cycle and market-cycle continue onward as a virtuous-circle.

But if we break off before that point, and only ever take the quick-profit short-cut, it also breaks the continuity of the virtuous-circle. For the Market-Cycle, what happens is that there's nothing there to maintain and reaffirm trust: which means that, if slowly at first, there's also a steady erosion of respect, and then of attention too – which eventually means no market, and no transactions. For the Story-Cycle, the short-cut also breaks the links with strategy, and hence also with any means to adapt to any changes in context; what tends to happen next is that existing tactics are re-used as a thin substitute for strategy – hence the infamous pseudo-strategy of 'last year plus 10%'. Which in both cases means the slow, sad, self-inflicted suicide of the company – and yet no-one apparently able to understand what it was that went wrong...

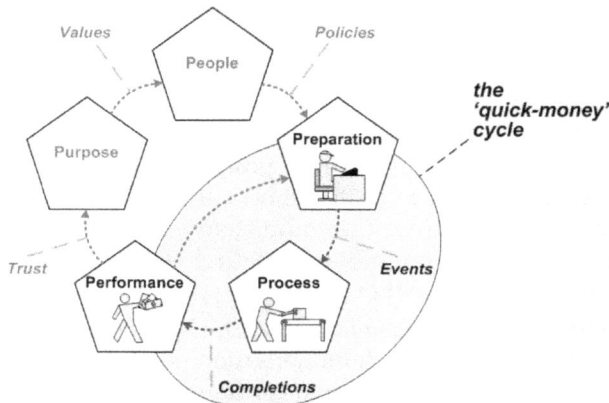

Figure 21: The 'quick-money' cycle

It's also possible to betray the story by accident, or by poor 'story-design'. This is one reason why mixing business-genres is riskier than it might at first seem. Each genre has its own 'rules', its own built-in expectations: if we mix genres, not only do we have two or more sets of 'rules' to satisfy, but in some cases the 'rules' will clash – which can make it almost impossible to satisfy everyone in that enterprise-space. It's doable, but definitely a delicate balance – and to make the story work, we *need* to know and respect all of those respective 'rules'.

All of this is why *governance* is so important – especially where that governance comes from beyond the organisation itself – because it helps the organisation maintain its links with the values of the broader shared-enterprise. Going back to that film example, note what we'll see listed right at the end of those credits: governance. Certifications from a whole swathe of external stakeholders, such as labour-unions, copyright-registries, auditors, health-and-safety, animal-welfare – that list goes on and on too.

Sometimes there'll be a happy spoof on this – "no pixels were harmed in the making of this movie" – but yes, even if the film is the most light-hearted of comedies, there's still a serious business behind it, with real responsibilities in the real world.

Responsibilities to the enterprise-vision.

Responsibilities to the story.

I just hope I'm holding to those same responsibilities here...

Application

- Within your organisation and enterprise, who are the good-guys, and the bad-guys? From whose point of view? Within which story, or version of the story? In what ways do those story-roles reverse as you shift the perspective of the story?

- If story is everywhere, who or what are the 'main-character' and 'impact-character' at each point in each story? What is the relationship between them at each point? In terms of the enterprise-story, what is it that drives that relationship? Which of those Dramatica archetype story-roles – protagonist, antagonist, reason, emotion, skeptic, sidekick, guardian, contagonist – does each take at each point in their interaction? How? And why?

- Who or what – if any – are your organisation's 'inherent anti-clients'? In what *architectural* ways could you change the story such that they could become allies rather than antagonists?

- By what means and mistakes would your organisation risk creating its own anti-clients, by 'betraying the story'? What *architectural* options do you have to reduce or mitigate those risks? What opportunities also arise for your organisation from those architectural options?
- What means do you have within the architecture to dissuade the organisation from falling into either of those two failure-modes – becoming overly self-centred within the story, and clinging on too long to the 'quick-profit' short-cut? What forms of governance would you need to support you in this? From where within the organisation or the broader-enterprise would that governance arise?

15: START AGAIN

A stark realisation: I've been doing this all wrong, haven't I?

I've betrayed the story. So far this hasn't been much about story: most of it has been about some kind of structure.

To be fair, mostly the structure of story, but structure nonetheless. And the whole point of this is that it's not about the structure: it's about the *story*. Story *as* story. Not structure.

So: start again, I guess.

Even this late in the story…

Okay, so it's about the story. Just the story – nothing else.

But now that I know it's about the story, what do I *do*? What do I need to do that's different from how I already do my enterprise-architecture?

A business-strategy document – that's already a kind of story, isn't it? If we focus more on story, that would be different how?

Who's going to use that story? What are they going to do with it? How will a focus on story make their work any better, any easier?

If strategy is a story, how should I use story at the operational level? Stories of operations, of business-transformation, or process, or purpose: what are these stories? How do they work? What's the point or purpose of each of these stories? What's the use, the value, the ROI even? What *is* the story?

Stories of what? Stories of the 'what', I guess; stories of where, when, which, who, how, why, and how they all link together with each other, interweave through each other. And story at every level of abstraction, from big-picture enterprise-vision right the way down to the fine-detail at each individual moment of action.

The gap between strategic intent and actual projects: the story of that gap, the stories of how those stories interrelate, linking to the overall story of the enterprise.

The story of each distinct context, about the details of that specific context: what's different here? What's the same? What's shared with other contexts, the same and the different? There are stories here: what are they?

The story of the enterprise: what's shared by everyone here? What *isn't* shared by everyone, and why, and how? In what ways does this one enterprise differ from every other? What stays the same? What's the story where each enterprise connects and interweaves with every other enterprise in that space?

What stories support the conversations and connections between enterprise-architect, solution-architect, designer, implementer and everyone else involved in implementing the architecture?

So many stories… Where once there seemed to be no stories at all, no role or reason for story, suddenly story is *everywhere*.

But if story is everywhere, where do we start? And how?

Application

- What happens for you when you hit up against some 'Dark Night of the Soul' in your own enterprise-architecture work? If the 'dark night' is a story that's gotten stuck in a loop somehow, how do you change the story, to break free?
- When faced with an overload of information, where do you start? Amidst all that clutter and chaos, how do you create enough of a story to help you get started?

16: START ANYWHERE

A happier realisation: if everything's connected to everything else, then it doesn't much matter *where* I start. Anywhere will do: what matters is that I *do* get started.

So: start anywhere.

(Interesting how challenging that statement is – like the writer's fear of that blank sheet of paper…)

Start with the first thing that comes to mind… just *do* it…

The locksmith: that'll do, I guess.

This is from an EA consultancy gig some years back, working with a large logistics firm. We'd done all the usual process-models and capability-maps and the like. Thought we'd covered everything. And then one day, as I walked towards the office, I noticed a small van with the company logo, parked close to one of the streetside collection-boxes. Yet it wasn't a standard mail-collection van, so I took a closer look – and it turned out to be the locksmith.

The *locksmith*.

Of course.

So easy to miss their part of the story. They hadn't appeared on any of our models because there were so few of them – only one or two at most in each state. But they're absolutely essential to the whole enterprise: if the collection-guys can't get the box open, the entire business-model grinds to a halt, 'cos that mail ain't goin' no further than the street.

(Okay, there's a famous FedEx story about that, about the driver who took the whole box in the van instead when he'd left the keys at the depot – but they still needed the keys at the other end to open the box when they got there.)

Without a working lock, the box won't open. Or, just as worrying, the box won't close. And that latter point was the real reason why the locksmith was on staff, rather than just another outsourced service: one of those cases where security has priority over short-term profit. A core part of the company's business-model was a government contract for mail: and a key condition in that contract was that access to a collection-box would never pass outside the company's control. By definition, any outsourcing-arrangement means that some parts of the service are on the far side of the organisation's boundary-of-control: but to comply with the mail-contract, control of access to each box – the locks and keys – must stay *within* that boundary-of-control. Hence, in turn, for the company's means to maintain those keys and locks: the locksmith.

That one incident – an unexpected oddity noticed in passing, and the conversation that followed – sent me off on an urgent hunt for other 'unsung heroes', both in that organisation and in others ever since. And often that search has highlighted a subtle yet scarily-serious gap somewhere within the architecture – though some-times only via a Joni-Mitchell-style 'you don't know what you've got till it's gone'... Most often these were to do with odd specialist skills or non-IT knowledge: like the only guy who knew how to regrind worn tram-wheels round again so they wouldn't trash the tracks; or the young woman with the blurry job-title who turned out to be the 'super-node' of the social-network for the bank's emergency-response team; or the only guy in the country who knew the safe method to make detonators and other primary-explosives.

None of these were wise people to lose: but it happens far too often, especially when someone tries to 'save money' in the short-term by getting rid of supposedly-'unimportant' people, without thinking enough about the deeper consequences of doing so.

The same applies to many supposedly-redundant systems that are scattered throughout the enterprise: time and again we've found some business-critical process dependent on a single spreadsheet maintained by one person on one ancient and easily-lost laptop, with no alternate, no documentation and no backup. Ouch...

So this again is where enterprise-architecture can save the day, by showing what the consequences of loss or damage would be. But it can only do that if the architecture goes into enough depth to describe what it is that all these 'unimportant' people and systems actually do...

The moral of this tale? Respect all those small-stories, because they always connect somewhere to the larger ones that really matter. Be ready to start anywhere, and keep eyes open for unexpected oddities – then follow the story wherever it leads.

Application

- If everything's connected to everything else, and you can start the story of your architecture anywhere, where would you choose to start? What immediate idea or image arises in response to that question? What do you discover if you *do* start at that initial 'anywhere'?

- Who are the 'unsung heroes' of your organisation, who hold the enterprise-story together in some crucial yet often-unnoticed way? As you follow their stories, what do you discover about risks and risk-mitigation, business-continuity and disaster-recovery planning, and even new opportunities and options to do the work in a different and better way?

- What's your own experience of a 'you don't know what you've got till it's gone', within your own organisation or in its broader enterprise? How much did it cost, in time, money and effort, to replace what was lost? What do you need to do, *within the architecture*, to ensure that it doesn't happen again?

INTERLUDE

Frustration in spades... I'm going crazy here, trying to find *any* viable way to use my existing enterprise-architecture tools to do this story-work. Those tools are great for the structure side; but there's almost nothing for the more narrative, free-form side of the story, and even less to help us bring those two sides together. Which, in practice, is a serious problem, because the *story* is what engages people in the architecture...

In short, we need our EA toolsets to help us bring a better balance between structure and story in the architecture, and provide us with better support for what we actually *do*. For example, try out these straightforward scenarios:

-- *Scenario 1*: The team reckon they've done well with their work on the new business-model, all laid out on the wall on a Business Model Canvas. But how are they going to implement it? Will it actually work in real-world practice? What are the pitfalls and hidden 'gotchas' that could cripple the new model's viability?

To address these concerns, they set up a review-session using a requirements-method called 'This', which feeds into architecture-modelling with Enterprise Canvas. One of the architecture-team leads, Maria, takes on the role of modeller, using an application on her tablet-computer, the screen hooked up to a data-projector on the wall, but also coupled to the other team-members' tablets and laptops. (The screen will also show the current manually-selected or randomly-selected 'This' question-card.) She also sets up a conference-microphone to capture an audio-channel.

Maria uses the camera on her tablet to take a snapshot of the current model on Business Model Canvas, and pulls the photo into the application. There, she marks up the graphic with zones and links, each of which – behind the scenes – is also noted as a Service or flow-relation in the underlying Enterprise Canvas.

The team choose an arbitrary starting-point, and build outward from there, as per the guidelines for the game. Instead of using the rather sparse Enterprise Canvas notation, Maria pulls up more-descriptive icons and images from a palette – trucks, parcels, people, machines, money, whatever – and places them on the screen as the current 'This'-item. Behind the scenes, though, the application stores the information in Enterprise Canvas notation. The audio-channel is attached both to the overall model, and to the entity for the current 'This'; later, the audio-track can be played back, highlighting in matching sequence each of the items described in the model.

During the game, the discussion indicates that some changes will need to be made to the initial business-model. Maria uses the underlying Enterprise Canvas to recreate a new version of that model, in Business Model Canvas layout.

-- *Scenario* 2: Two days after the business-model meeting, Maria reviews some of the people-connections that were captured in the Enterprise Canvas model during the 'This'-session, to build a list of stakeholders for one of the side-projects arising from the new business-model. She notices that she didn't capture one person's name, the process-owner for a related business-process – she remembers that his first-name was Steve, but not the surname. She clicks on the respective icon, and plays back the audio-channel that was captured at the time: Steve's surname – Cartwright – is now clear, and she types the full name into the model. As she does so, a link with the company's HRM-system brings up further contact-details for Steve, including some photographs. She selects one photo, and sets it as the surface-view for that service-entity in Enterprise Canvas.

Later that day, Arjun also reviews the business-model, using the zooming model-display. In the drill-down into the *Key Activities* section of the Business Model Canvas, Steve's photograph now appears in place of the previous abstract 'person'-icon. Clicking on the photograph, Arjun sees all of the information on Steve's role in the proposed business-model, and can also play back the captured audio both from that meeting, and from another discussion that took place earlier in the day.

-- *Scenario* 3: Juan has been tasked with developing the IT-architecture for the e-commerce component of the new business-model. His business-unit has standardised on Archimate notation for all IT-architecture models. He opens the Enterprise Canvas model, and, using it as an active backplane, identifies Canvas entities that would map directly to Archimate equivalents: Canvas *Service* to Archimate *Business Service, Application Service* or *Infrastructure Service*; Canvas *Exchange* to Archimate *Business Interface, Business Object* and so on. He explores the other details recorded in the 'This' session to identify Archimate entities such as *Business*

Function, Business Event, Business Actor and the like. As he adds these entities to the Archimate model, they're also attached to the underlying Enterprise Canvas model via composition-relation links into the respective Canvas *Service* and *Exchange* entities and flow-relations.

-- **Scenario 4**: The following morning, one of the business-model team, Vasily, remembers that more detail was needed about the warehouse configuration, for potential locations – both physical and logical – for the new sensors that will be needed for logistics-tracking within the new business-model. He goes down to the warehouse, takes his smartphone out of his pocket, calls up the Enterprise Canvas model, selects the 'New Sensors' *Service*-entity, and starts a new session of 'This' with that entity as its starting-point. He manually selects the question 'What are the locations of This?'; he then attaches to that card the photos that he takes, direct from the phone's camera application.

In the Enterprise Canvas, Juan has already been identified as one of the people responsible for the 'New Sensors' component of the business-model. He receives a notification that new items have been added to the Enterprise Canvas; he opens that part of the model, reviews it, and adds new entities to his Archimate model, which are automatically linked back to the Enterprise Canvas.

So there we are: some typical scenarios on using EA-tools to link structure and story, to guide the overall enterprise-architecture.

Plenty of other scenarios we could add, too: about a meetup in a cafe, about people exchanging ideas in the elevator, about how this information might be used by a project-manager and her team, by a process-designer to gather feedback from the factory floor, by managers using a dashboard in high-level resource-planning, and so on. But enough detail for now: four interlinked scenarios, all working on the same models in different ways, with different software applications, on different hardware platforms, for different purposes, all supporting each other.

So is that what actually happens in practice at present? Is that how we can use existing EA tools in our everyday architecture work?

Uh, no…

In which case, why not?

Seriously: *why not?*

On the surface, it's all straightforward enough: the work itself is essentially what architects and others do already. The only trouble is that it's well-nigh impossible to do most of this in any existing EA toolset. It's true that most tools now would cope with the Archimate-specific part of the modelling, on a desktop or laptop platform, but that's about it – and they probably wouldn't be able to link any of that model to anything else, on any other toolset, or onto any other platform. As for the rest, using freeform images, video, audio, tablets, smartphones? – well, forget it, guys, you're outta luck…

Ouch…

It *should* all be seamless, pretty much exactly as described in those scenarios above. In practice, it isn't. In fact, the way we have to do it right now is a frustration-filled, kludge-ridden, error-prone mess of manual translation, bits of paper, scribbled notes, emails, anguished phone-calls and worse. Ridiculous. Hence no surprise that it often doesn't work well – if at all.

Yet there really is no need for it to be that way, and no reason for it to *be* that way either.

To which the only remaining question is: *Why*? Why is it still this way? And can't we do it better than this? Please?

Application

- What enterprise-architecture toolsets do you use? On which platforms? For what purposes?

- How well do those toolsets serve your needs? What happens when you try to use those tools to explain architectural ideas to non-technical folk?

- Who else uses those tools? Perhaps more to the point, who *doesn't* use those tools? What happens if you *do* allow inexperienced executives and the like to be let loose on your models through those tools?

- What do you use for all the other types of architecture-modelling that can't be done through those tools – from freeform sketches to voice-capture and video-annotation? How – if at all – do you link that other work into the maintained architecture-models?

- Given those answers, what to you would be your ideal toolset for enterprise-architecture? And what can *you* do, perhaps, to help make that happen?

17: PUT MYSELF IN THE STORY

I really need to stop struggling with this. All it takes is a bit of imagination, a memory or two; people, places, a few 'tales of the unexpected'. Where we were; where we are; where we need to be. That'll do it.

So: put myself in this story – this shared-enterprise of enterprise-architecture.

Like all good stories, this one starts a long way back – almost forty years, in fact. Studying graphic design at art-college in London, which also included a brief stint at the Architectural Association. I didn't seem to fit in with any of the usual design-categories, and no-one quite knew where to put me, either, so I kind of ended up at the Royal College of Art, doing a Masters Degree in General Studies, going across just about every discipline going, in order to do a thesis on design for skills-education. Which worked well enough – the book that came out of it was a brief best-seller, anyway. What that really did define for me, though, was a lifelong interest in meta-methodology and method – which has become a lot more important in the past decade. But I'm getting ahead of the story, of course – as stories do tend to do.

Then a fair few years 'doing my time' on software development, trying to find ways to link the then very-new microcomputers to the even newer breed of phototypesetting machines, to create the first viable version of what later became desktop-publishing. All of that code written in assembly-language, by the way: megabytes of it. Not trivial. And neither was the struggle of re-thinking and re-structuring an entire discipline, almost from scratch – something I seem to have done several times now in my aptly-named 'career'.

Then a literally-erratic drift from place to place and even continent to continent, doing all manner of odd bits of consultancy and trouble-shooting: one more-memorable example was sorting out a misbehaving robot truck in a toothpaste-factory, in the midst of a tornado, somewhere in the middle of the Midwest. Finally, for a while, ending up doing database-design in a research-laboratory down in southern Australia – a place we nicknamed the RSPCA, 'the Royal Society for the Promotion of Cruelty to Airframes'.

It was there that I came across a guy called Graeme Burnett, who's been a real influence on the way I think about information. Data is useless on its own: to know what it *means*, we need to know its context, and its connections to everything else. As Graeme put it:

> We need every item to answer two questions: tell me about yourself, and tell me what you're associated with.

It's an interesting data-challenge, because rather than merely the relatively-simple many-to-many database-relationship, we need to support true any-to-any relations – and still keep track of what's going on. I just wish that some of the current crop of enterprise-architecture toolsets could do this...

The next data-challenge was at a telco, working with a team led by Bob McDowell, a wonderfully wry guy with a truly encyclopaedic knowledge of the industry and all its foibles. Again consultancy, this time for a major transformation of the business, and my part of it was doing the data-modelling. Except that it wasn't just the usual mapping of logical-to-physical and the like: this was about mapping the *business* use of information, which is a completely different ballgame, tracking all the transforms, and the *people* as well as the systems that were involved at each stage. The eTOM framework (now called Frameworx) was a happy discovery: an enterprise-architecture framework from folks who really *did* understand a business-world beyond just IT alone. But oh, the joys of trying to disentangle all those business-critical processes that depended on undocumented, unsupported, out-of-date spread-sheets. Again. Sigh...

Another dubiously unjoyful discovery there: the ways in which even the best-planned business-transformation can be brought to a futile halt by the absurdities of an inane accounting-model. In this case, the business-case for the whole project depended on being able to show cost-savings from shutting down old redundant IT-systems. The catch was that only a handful of large systems were listed individually in the accounts: everything else was lumped together under a single line-item of 'Other'. That meant that whilst the decommissioning-costs would show up in the accounts, there was no way to demonstrate the savings, because they all vanished into that all-consuming 'Other'. Result: no business-case – so we never did get the chance to finish the job. And tens of millions still wasted every year, just because the accounting-system made no sense. Also sigh...

It would have been somewhen around then that I first met Shawn Callahan, at some kind of Melbourne meetup for knowledge-management folk. Back then he was still with IBM, their KM lead for Asia-Pacific, but he was soon to move out on his own, to set up his strategic-story consultancy Anecdote. Sitting there in the grubby front-room at Cooper's Inn, on the corner of Lonsdale and Exhibition in the Melbourne central business district, we scribbled diagrams in notebooks and compared our various sensemaking-models, me with a simple Jung-inspired frame I'd worked on since the early '80s, he with a useful-looking framework that these days, sadly, I dare not even name. No matter: the real point is that from Shawn I've learnt a great deal about story and the business-role of story, and I still learn more about the value of that work every day. Hence, in no small part, this book.

Then next was another business-transformation, for a nationwide logistics firm. It was through Helen Mills and her team there that I learnt a lot about whole-of-enterprise context, and about the limit-ations of conventional IT-centric 'enterprise'-architecture. So much so, in fact, that we ended up taking over the existing enterprise-architecture department, politely moving most of that team back to IT where they belonged (and where they were much happier anyway). We had to do a lot of work on frameworks, first with FEAF, and then with TOGAF, trying to find something that was actually usable for a real-world enterprise-architecture context: we never did find a way to get their notions of 'business-architecture' to make sense to anyone beyond IT. Which is why we ended up 'rolling our own', always with a focus on the architecture of the organisation and enterprise *as a unified whole*.

Which is why, when I moved back to Europe some years ago, it was a bit of a shock to discover that the enterprise-architecture world over here was still stuck in the drear days of IT-centrism. Oh dear.

But that, as they say, is another story. Time to move on to another part of the story for now, perhaps?

Application

- What's *your* story? Where you do place your own history and experience within the overall disciplines of enterprise-architecture and the like? What have you learned throughout the years?

- Who are the people who've influenced you most in your work in enterprise-architectures? What have you learnt from them? What are the stories there?
- In what ways and what contexts have you applied what you learnt from those people? And how have you passed on that knowledge and experience to others?
- What have you contributed so far to the broader enterprise of enterprise-architecture? What more can you add to the story of this discipline as a whole?

18: THE STORY-DOCTORS

In an industry beset with strange job-titles – best boy, gaffer, key grip, foley-artist and so many more – there's one role you'll rarely see included in that long, long list of credits at the end of the film: story-doctor. Yet despite their apparent invisibility, they're some of Hollywood's most important unsung heroes – because without their work, even the greatest of stories might never have made it to the screen at all.

So what does a story-doctor do? Part of it is about plugging the plot-holes, cleaning up character-arc, simplifying the set-ups and sequences and suchlike. But mostly it's about making sure that the architecture of the story works as a unified whole, all the way from the big-picture strategy of the storyworld, right down to the fine details of storyweaving and story-execution.

In that sense it's a lot like enterprise-architecture. We search for plot-holes too, though we're more likely to think of them just as gaps in the overall architecture. And although there's the surface picture, the grand scheme that everyone sees, most of the real work is all but invisible: all that subtle structure of services and systems that holds everything together behind the scenes.

Much as for the story-doctor, often the most important part of the work is preventive, catching problems *before* they occur. It's very easy to see mistakes, very hard to make sure they don't happen in the first place: hence one of the hardest parts of proving the value of what we do is that the better we do our work, the less there is to be seen. Tricky, that…

To see what a story-doctor actually does, we only have to wander around in the websites that list the originals of various filmscripts, and compare those to the final versions. An eye-opener indeed…

One of my favourites for this is a mid-ranking romantic-comedy called *Kate & Leopold*, which uses a time-travel motif to set up the inevitable 'fish out of water' theme. The original version is a truly awful cliché-ridden mess, including yet another clunky rehash of the Cinderella story. Yet the script that underpins the final film is really quite good: a huge improvement, certainly. In essence, it's still much the same story, yet this time there's hardly a cliché in sight; even that *deus-ex-machina* time-machine disappears from view. In its place, there's a taut if still somewhat-simple storyline, some nice comedic action and dialogue, and also some *very* nicely acerbic asides about present-day values and worldviews. There's a good cast, too, which definitely helps – though that's not part of the script itself, of course.

To me, the most interesting part of that film is not the story, or the actors, or the costumes or set. It's that *someone* had done a quietly brilliant job of tidying up that initial mess, changing an abysmal bad-joke of a first-draft script into something that really did work. That's a story-doctor.

So what do enterprise-architects do? We're story-doctors for the enterprise-story: we plug the plot-holes, find and fix the flaws and follies, bridge across all those separated silos...

And much as with those filmscripts, the real source of so many of those problems is a failure to think *systemically*, a failure to think always in terms of the whole, balancing the story-detail with the big-picture of the enterprise storyworld. In practice, this usually comes out as a particularly maddening myopia that we could summarise as '*something*-centrism'.

Courtesy of some unfortunate flaws in many of the major EA frameworks, the most common form of 'something-centrism' at present is IT-centrism – the belief that everything must begin and end with IT, an imaginary world centred solely around computer-based information. One personal example:

> A formal review-meeting with an ardent young database-designer, working on the current project to create single-source-of-truth for asset-management. Nice IT-architecture, nice data-modelling, a clean mapping of logical-to-physical, all the rest. But I couldn't see any mention of data-quality, or the myriad of other sub-systems and support-processes needed for real-world information-management. No user-interface to do any of that work, for that matter.

> "Why would we need any of that?" he asked, obviously perplexed. "It's all in the database, isn't it?"

> I reassured him that his data-design was good work, as far as it went.

> "So what's the problem? If I have record of a chair in the database, that's the same as the chair. No difference."

> Turned out he had no idea what a stocktake was, or an inventory-check; it'd never occurred to him that things might

go missing, or that the record and the real-world object might not line up with each other. Oops…

Or another example, at an EA conference:

"Why are you so anti-IT?" he said. "IT is the centre of everything – no modern business can run without it!"

"But what if it has to?" I asked. "What happens when that IT is out of action? That's the whole point of business-continuity: being able to keep going, whatever's going on. It's not 'anti-IT' to say that our architecture needs to cover that kind of context too, surely?"

He wasn't convinced. "So what? Just harden the IT", he said. "It'll keep running."

"Under ten feet of floodwater, when there's no outside power-supply, and no-one can get to the data-centre to maintain it? Have you *any* idea how much that kind of IT will cost you – if you can get it to work at all? Have you tried making a business-case to the executive for that kind of money?"

He at last started to look a bit more worried.

"Don't you think there might be cheaper, simpler ways to do it?" I said. "Ones that might not necessarily involve IT?"

He jerked back, almost in horror. "Ridiculous! IT is the centre of modern business!" he all but shouted. "No business can run without it!"

I gave up at that point, and politely walked away…

Yet it's not just IT-centrism that's the problem here: increasingly we have to deal with 'business-centrism' too:

More mockery from the business-brigade. "You're stupid, you know that? Forget anything else, shareholder-value is the only thing that matters. If you don't put shareholder-value at the centre of your models, it's pink-slip time."

A brief moment, then, for me to reflect that at times there are indeed some real advantages to *not* being an employee… and then back to the fray. "Sure: but where do you think the shareholder-value comes from?"

"Profit."

A brief silent sigh on my part. "And where do you think the profit comes from?"

"Money, of course. Are you a complete idiot?"

110

Another perhaps less-silent sigh. "So where do you think the money comes from? Profit is an *output*, not an *input*: you can't use money itself as a guide for the architecture-design. It's an outcome of a whole bunch of non-linear, non-reversible transforms, and almost all of them link back to values other than money. So that's where the architecture starts – with the enterprise-values, not money."

"Bullshit. Only thing that matters is money." A sarcastic sneer: "Enjoy your pink-slip, bub!"

The company went out of business six months later, killed by a catastrophic collapse in customer-confidence. So pink-slip time for everyone, including those business-architects; but they never did quite notice the connection there…

And, of course, there was that 'rising star' of the junior-executive, full of hungry ambition, and ambitious plans to match:

Sharp face, sharp voice, sharp suit. He'd commanded us to attend a presentation of his proposed New Way Of Working – the capital-letters were definitely there – and we sat in horror as he proudly displayed his utter absence of any architectural awareness.

Or human awareness, for that matter: "See? We can get rid of at least a thousand workers there – and another couple of thousand over here too. Redundant: we don't need them any more. We can replace them all with machines."

He seemed not to know that those machines didn't actually exist – they were just vapourware on a brochure he'd seen somewhere. He also had no idea that those front-line staff that he'd so airily dismissed were the key source for data-quality: without them, our core backbone-data would become meaningless within months. We told him this, but he was in no mood to listen:

"You talk about alignment? I have the ear of the board on this: I don't have to align to your architecture, you have to align to *me*!"

He was fired soon after, fortunately, before he'd had much more of a chance to do irreparable damage to the business…

As a story-doctor, we'll need a good 'bedside-manner' – in other words, the real importance of tact, diplomacy and all those other so-called 'soft-skills' that are often so hard in practice… (Gerry Weinberg's *Secrets of Consulting* books have been a real life-saver there…) At times, though, we'll need to be willing, and able, to give some client a good hard kick to wake them up to what's really going on – no matter how little they want to listen. And we also need the quiet acceptance that, no matter how competent our advice may be, often the ultimate decision for action is not ours to make: hence back to the narrative-paradigm again, and why it's so important to ensure that 'rational' reasons are experienced as 'good reasons' too.

Anyway, perhaps the most crucial point here is that, in any true enterprise-architecture, *everything and nothing is 'the centre', all at the same time*. If we fail to grasp that point, or what it means in practice, our architecture will be on a guaranteed path to failure too: it really *is* that important. 'You Have Been Warned', etcetera?

Going back to the story-doctor, another key point is that the story can change all the way through the production-cycle. The script is not a static thing, a '*the* architecture of the story'; and just as with enterprise-architecture, working on that script is rarely just a one-time transition from current-state to future-state. It's *emergent* – with everything that that implies.

A film-production may well have 'a cast of thousands' – most of whom will never appear in front of a camera. Yet almost all of those people will want their voice to be heard in the story, in one way or another – and it's important that their voice *is* heard, because they each bring something new to the story. Which means that the story will change in some way or other, every time: it's emergent. And whilst the director always has the responsibility for the overall story, it's often the story-doctor who keeps the screenplay in shape, keeping it on-track to the vision throughout all of those changes.

Hence, in turn, the enterprise-architect, as enterprise 'story-doctor' – working with that 'cast of thousands' to create an architecture that actually works, in true support of the enterprise vision.

Interesting work, isn't it? – *if* we can somehow stay sane under the strain…!

Application

- As a 'story-doctor' for the enterprise-story – or, more usually, your organisation's involvement in that enterprise-story – what are some of the 'plot-holes' that you've had to find and fix? What kind of awareness did you need in order to be able to find them?

- When faced with "an abysmal bad-joke" of an initial architecture, where do you start? And once you've started as the architecture's 'story-doctor', from where do you find the commitment to keep you going?

- What are your experiences of 'something-centrism'? In each case, what was the area that was presumed to be 'the centre of everything'? What did you need to do in order to resolve the narrowness, and open it up to a more inclusive architectural view?

- Who was the perpetrator of that 'something-centrism'? What did or could you do to get them to connect with that broader view? If *you* were the perpetrator – and it's probable all of us have been so, from time to time – what did and could you do, in order to be able to 'think wider' once more? Given that, what can you learn from that personal experience, in order to help others break out of *their* respective box?

- What 'soft-skills' do you need in your work as an enterprise-architect? From where and how do you learn them? How do you balance those 'soft-skills' with the 'hard-skills' and technical competence you need within your architecture?

- How do you ensure that everyone's voice is heard appropriately within the architecture? How do you keep the balance between all of the competing voices, and still keep everything aligned to the overall vision?

- How easy – or hard – is it for you to let go control of the architecture? What do you need to do to accept that ultimately it *isn't* your responsibility?

INTERLUDE

Talking of the 'story-doctor' reminds me not only of architecture, but of the everyday doctor too.

My parents first met when they were both medical students in London during the Blitz. When they qualified, just after the end of that war, they chose to go into general practice (what Americans would term a 'family-doctor'). At the time, general practitioners often did quite a bit of hospital medicine, working alongside the specialist consultants; but when the National Health Service was set up, a few years later, those two domains of medicine were split apart. From then on, specialism was supposedly the only way to get ahead: general-practitioners were almost despised, as failures who'd "fallen off Moran's ladder". It wasn't a happy time…

Yet in many ways, general-practice is probably the most *real* form of medicine. Where a hospital-specialist would see much the same thing, over and over, with only minor variations, my parents saw huge variety in that rural practice in southern England. There was the cowherd with anthrax, for example – a disease so virulent that it's now classed as biological warfare. There was the middle-aged woman who 'felt a bit faint' after an insect-bite in the garden, and who only survived because my mother got there faster than the ambulance could. And there was that other elderly woman, sent home from hospital to spend her last days with her family, whose supposed terminal cancer turned out instead to be, uh, something *much* simpler, and that could be cured by repeated dose of a really powerful laxative… and she lived on, in good health and happily unhindered digestion, for many years more.

In short, an interesting world. One that must cope with anything that Reality Department cares to throw its way – and can do so *because* of that generalist breadth.

Which is the point here, really – particularly in relation to that analogy with architecture. What I see in enterprise-architecture in current organisations are three distinct modes of practice:

- *specialist-only*: deep domain-experience in a single domain – typical of solution-architects assigned on a per-project basis

- *'T-shaped'*: deep domain-experience in one domain, with some experience across others – typical of domain-architects who link across multiple projects
- *true generalist*: emphasis on breadth rather than depth, with some experience across *all* domains – typical (and even mandatory) for enterprise-architects

True generalists do indeed have a specialism: they specialise in being a generalist. For example, they have to learn the basics of new skills and new developments *really* fast – much faster than anyone else. They have to be able to 'translate' between *any* of the domains in scope – unlike a specialist, who, if they so choose, may well remain within one domain and its 'language' for the whole of their career. It's a very different set of skills than those of most other specialists.

But the catch is that, just as with the general-practitioner, there's not much respect for those generalist skills. As I know to my cost, the generalist always seems to come off second-best whenever we're compared to a specialist – which is a bit unfair, because I've often actually done *more* work than the specialist would.

Somehow we need to get more recognition and respect for what the generalist does. My parents played quite a major role in regaining that kind of recognition for general-practitioners in Britain; I guess it's my turn now, to work with other generalists to do much the same for the discipline of whole-enterprise architecture – because without it, this profession ain't goin' to go very far.

Looks like we might have a bit of a fight on our hands. Oh well...

Application

- How do you see your role and experience as an enterprise-architect: specialist, 'T-shaped' or generalist?
- If you're more of a generalist, how do you stand up for your worth in a culture that still over-values specialism?
- What can *you* do to improve the profile of generalists in enterprise-architecture and all the overall disciplines with which it connects?

19: WIN WITHOUT THE FIGHT

If this was a Hero's Journey type of story, this is the place where there would be the big final conflict, what gamers describe as 'the boss-fight'.

But I ain't no hero, and I don't want a fight. I've had more than enough of those already…

Which means I need to find some way to win here, but without the fight. And I only know one way I can get that to happen:

- hold to the shared-story
- make sure everyone wins

Yeah, I know: probably sounds crazy, wildly optimistic and such. And I'll also admit I'm definitely afraid here of being dismissed as some kind of nutcase, 'the crazy-man of enterprise-architecture'. (Okay, I may already have that kind of reputation in some places, especially with a few of the folks from the IT-oriented side of the story…) But what else *can* we do about this story of enterprise-architecture? Fight about it, may the best thug win? – is that really the best we can do? We do need to do better than that…

Which is what this is all about, really: creating the win without the fight. Not conflict, but the constructive tension in the shared-story. And everyone wins.

There's an old Quaker expression that it's hard to find the courage to fight, but even harder to *not* fight when we can. So how do we not-fight about this? Where do we start?

I suggest we start with a story.

A story about structure, that's also about story. A story about the architecture of the architecture.

I've done enterprise-architecture in a dozen different industries by now – maybe more. And over the years and decades I've been to a lot of conferences and the like. Yet what I've looking for, for all of this time, has been a story that helps me make sense of enterprise-architecture.

What *is* enterprise-architecture? What's the *story* here?

116

So many different stories; so many different views into one overall story. And so far it seems to me that the common core in all of those stories is one simple straightforward aim:

- *make things work better by working together, on purpose*.

It does seem to make sense as a vision-descriptor: everyone in this enterprise is focussed on the ways that things work; what we do is about reviewing and changing the way things work; and we want them to work better, more 'on purpose'. Focus; action; qualifier: it fits. But once we move down from that most abstract level? – ah, that's where things start to get messy…

To me the real problem is that the whole enterprise is riddled with 'something-centrism'. And whenever that happens, the Why gets conflated into the How and the What, such that that 'something' becomes its own purpose. Which, to my mind, kind of loses the plot and the point: the story no longer works as a whole, because it's literally lost its purpose.

Within current enterprise-architecture, the most dominant form of 'something-centrism' is IT-centrism. It's embedded right at the roots of just about every major taxonomy and framework – FEAF, TOGAF, Zachman – and in related notations such as Archimate. (There are a few EA-frameworks around that aren't inherently IT-centric, such as DoDAF, eTOM and TRAK, but they tend to be domain-specific or less well known.) IT-centrism is so dominant in enterprise-architecture at present that, to many people, EA is *only* about IT, and the fabled 'IT/business-alignment'.

Yet the reality, and the problem, is that there's a *lot* more to any enterprise-architecture than just its IT. Even if our only interest is in the IT, we need to understand all of its context in order to make the IT work better and on-purpose – and that context will usually extend not just to the whole organisation, but far beyond it into the broader shared-enterprise as well. IT-centrism, and any other form of 'something-centrism', makes its EA-story too small a story to work.

At least I'm not alone in this critique. For example, Len Fehskens of The Open Group has long challenged other members on this: he points out that by almost any measure, IT represents only a very small percentage of most organisations, so it makes no sense that it should demand almost all of the attention.

Yet whenever we bring up this point, at conferences and the like, there's always the same response (or accusation, perhaps): if we won't place IT as the centre of everything, we must be ignoring its role entirely. A strange black-and-white view of everything, when the reality is a lot more complex, and a lot more colourful. So of course IT is an important part of the enterprise, and obviously *must* be included within its overall architecture. But *not* as the sole centre of everything. And we also *must* include other aspects of the enterprise that may not touch IT at all (such as when the IT itself goes out of action) – otherwise we won't have an *enterprise-architecture*.

As Andrew McAfee once said about his so-called 'Enterprise 2.0', "it's not not about the technology". But it's also not *only* about the technology – and *that's* the point that so often gets missed. We're not 'anti-IT' for questioning IT-centrism: such accusations are not only pointless, but create a fight that none of us need...

I look back at the comment that started off this whole exploration – "there's no place anywhere in [that EA-framework] for people" – and straight away I'm reminded of Gerry Weinberg, in his *Secrets of Consulting*:

> Whatever it looks like, no matter how technical it seems, it's *always* a 'people-problem'.

Perhaps the real danger of IT-centrism and the like is that, whilst technology-challenges are rarely easy, in many ways the technical side is the easy bit of the overall context. At the least, technologies do tend to follow a linear logic: in most cases there *are* distinct, definite, repeatable solutions to each of its problems. Not so with most 'people-problems': often packed full of uncertainty, inherent unpredictability, wicked-problems and other chaotic confusions – and none of them easy at all.

I do sometimes wonder how much people choose to take on the hard technical challenges as a way to avoid dealing with the *really* hard human ones... But for a viable enterprise-architecture, we'll need to face *all* of the context – not solely a conveniently-selected subset. That to me is the real challenge here.

So what *does* it take to include people into enterprise-architecture? I hope I've made some solid start on that here: still with too much emphasis on structure, perhaps, but enough to start on for now. In reading back through this, it seems like I must've rambled all over the place: and yet it's clear to me now that all those interludes and digressions *are* part of the overall story. Anything that works with people does ramble all over the place: that's part of the nature of people, really. Like people, though unlike most structure, a story doesn't come together in nice neat logical sequence: it has its own rules, its own logic, and we have to work *with* them if we're to get useful results.

And also in reading back through this, what always seem to stand out are the stories – wherever there's a real person in that place, rather than abstract structure. Each structure is interesting, of course, and important, yet oddly also kind of deadening; it always needs a story to bring it to life. Yet story on its own doesn't work, either: it needs structure to, well, give it some structure, really. So we need both, and we need a good balance between both, too: structure *and* story, story *and* structure.

To make this work – to create stories that engage people in what happens in the architecture – we need to rewrite our *own* story, about this discipline of enterprise-architecture. And for that, we do already have the structure of story:

- the story-trigger – often as 'something unexpected happened'
- the people – or sometimes 'things-as-people'
- the place, and other context for the story
- the events, the conversation, the structure and sequence of 'what happened before' and 'what happened next'
- the 'moral of the story', the lessons-learned – or not-learned…

Story creates *engagement* in the story itself; and story is *everywhere*. Layer upon layer of story, and of story-within story, all the way from a low-level protocol-exchange between two web-services, to the person using the application that uses those services, to the business-process in which that person is engaged, to the business of the business itself, and the whole extended-enterprise in which it plays its part. They're all one story; they're many stories; they're all *stories*. Stories weaving through structure, as "a canvas for relaying societal myths, a stage for the theater of everyday life".

So how *do* we make our own enterprise work better, how *do* we work together on purpose? Seems to me that there's a story in there… a story from which *everyone* wins.

And that's a purpose worth fighting about.

Or, preferably, perhaps worth not-fighting about?

Application

- "Hold to the shared-story; make sure everyone wins": when you're faced with a situation that looks like turning into a fight, is that a way out that works for you? How *do* you resolve a conflict without destroying that useful tension that drives the story forward?

- What, to you, is the shared-enterprise of enterprise-architecture? What is it that comprises the storyworld and storymind of enterprise-architecture? What's the story?

- Who are the players in this enterprise of enterprise-architecture? What are their respective drivers? What are the shared vision, values and commitments that bind them all together? How do all the different visions and values intersect?

- "Make things work better by working together, on purpose": does that phrase work well for you, as a central unifying vision for enterprise-architecture"? If not, what would you change? What would be *your* choice? Why? And how and where and in what ways would you stand up for your choice?

- Who or what tends to dominate the enterprise-architecture story so far? Whose view of the story tends to be portrayed as '*the* story'? Given the dominance of that view, who tends to be portrayed as 'the good-guys' or 'the bad-guys'? Who is 'us', versus 'them'? By choosing to break free of '*the* story', in what ways do those portrayals of good-guys versus bad-guys shift and blur as you shift the view?

- What part do *you* play in this extended story? As the main-character in your part of this story, who or what would act as impact-character for you in that story? Within the overall story, which of the eight Dramatica archetype-roles do you tend to play: protagonist, antagonist, reason, emotion, skeptic, sidekick, guardian, contagonist? Given this, who or what takes on for you the other archetype-roles?

- What are the trade-offs and the priorities in the enterprise of enterprise-architecture? Who or what – if anyone - manages the governance of those trade-offs? How do we change the story, to create the win without the fight? What can *you* do to create the win without the fight?

- How much do you see people tackling only the technical issues, or pushing for technology-based 'solutions', as a way to avoid facing the much harder human issues? In what ways could you change the story, so as to make it easier to include the people-side within the architecture of the overall solution?

- Apply all of the above to your own organisation and enterprise: what's the story? What is it that binds everyone and everything together? What is it that comprises its storyworld and storymind? Who or what dominates the view of the story? Who are the 'good-guys' and 'bad-guys' in that view, and what happens to those perceptions as you shift the perspective into the story? What storylistening do you need to do so as to help others and yourself make sense of the story, and to change the story in line with shared aims and needs? What can *you* do, within and beyond your architecture, to create the win without the fight?

- What, for you, is "the story in there… a story from which everyone wins"? What's *your* part in that story? What can *you* do to help create an enterprise-story from which everyone wins?

20: WRAP UP THE STORY

Time to get back to the everyday world, I guess: there's a backlog of work that I need to get back to, and it won't wait around any longer. Sigh...

Some story, though. A story about story, that itself is a story.

The storytellers often talk at this point about 'the return with the elixir': returning from the sojourn in the 'special-world' with something new, something different, something that that makes a real difference for everyone. Somehow story seems to be a lot *quieter* than that: I don't know that I'd make any of it out to be so special, yet for me it's true there'd be a fair few themes here that might almost fit as 'the elixir of story':

- architecture is about structure, yet it's *also* about story
- story is always about *people*, in one sense or another
- story is what engages people in the aims of the enterprise – whatever that enterprise may be
- narrative provides a sequence of action in context – it becomes a story only when we add the *why*
- organisation focuses on structure, yet the enterprise *is* the story – the structure happens *because* of the story
- structures may be re-used in other stories – but the structure *itself* is not the story
- those random-seeming interludes and asides *are* part of the story – and often provide the most useful side of that story
- we don't control the story, and we don't possess it – it's more like *it* possesses *us*
- the story's over when it's over – and then it often starts again anyway

Just like structure, story is *everywhere* in enterprise-architecture – and just as important, too. Yet also just like structure, story isn't everything: it's just a story. We can use it, or not, as we need.

And that's really the point, perhaps: story is nothing special – it's just another tool in the enterprise-architect's toolkit. Might not have noticed it much before, but it's there now when we need it, and – like any good tool - it's useful when used in the right way.

So what would we do different on Monday morning, as a result of all of this? Maybe quite a lot, maybe nothing at all: it's up to each of us, really. Working with story can be a very different way of working: at the very least, it'll take some time to seep in to our way of *seeing*, the way we think about architectures in general. If we want, we can choose to stick with a classic structure-only view: there's nothing wrong in that, it's just a bit more limiting, that's all. If we do that, though, at least we do now know that the story-side is there and ready for us whenever we need it – and to make our architecture-work a lot more interesting, too.

See what happens on Monday morning, I guess: a different kind of story, perhaps?

Application

- What for you would be 'the elixir of story' for enterprise-architecture? What themes stood out for you as you read through this book?
- Which items could you use straight away in your enterprise-architecture toolkit? Which items would need more practice, or wait until some appropriate context comes along?
- And which items still seem to make no sense at all? In what ways are you willing to trust that they *will* make sense when the time is right, even if not before? What's the story behind that story?
- Given what you've seen here, what would you do differently come Monday morning, in your enterprise-architecture or elsewhere? And what stories do you need – or what *different* stories do you need – to ensure that you *can* do it differently on Monday morning?

APPENDIX: SOURCES AND RESOURCES

Sources

This a summary of the main references and sources mentioned in the text above. It's in alphabetical order, with books sorted by title rather than author.

- Matthew Frederick, *101 Things I Learned in Architecture School* (MIT Press, 2007)
- Archimate modelling-notation for enterprise-architecture: see Wikipedia, en.wikipedia.org/wiki/ArchiMate and Open Group, www.opengroup.org/archimate
- Business Model Canvas: see Wikipedia, en.wikipedia.org/wiki/Business_Model_Canvas; also Alex Osterwalder, Yves Pigneur et al., *Business Model Generation: a handbook for visionaries, game-changers and challengers* (self-published, 2010)
- Christopher Alexander, *A Pattern Language: Towns, Buildings, Construction* (Oxford University Press Press, 1977); also see Wikipedia, en.wikipedia.org/wiki/A_Pattern_Language
- BPMN (Business Process Modeling Notation): see Wikipedia, en.wikipedia.org/wiki/BPMN
- Chris Crawford, *Chris Crawford on Interactive Storytelling* (New Riders, 2005)
- Cluetrain Manifesto: see www.cluetrain.com
- 'Deadly-embrace' in systems-design: see Wikipedia, en.wikipedia.org/wiki/Deadlock
- DoDAF ([US] Department of Defense Architecture Framework): see Wikipedia, en.wikipedia.org/wiki/DoDAF
- Dramatica story-structure: see dramatica.com and storymind.com/dramatica; also Armando Saldaña-Mora, *Dramatica for Screenwriters* (Write Brothers, 2005)
- Enterprise as story (on Tetradian weblog): weblog.tetradian.com/the-enterprise-is-the-story
- Enterprise Canvas: see Tom Graves, *Mapping The Enterprise: modelling the enterprise as services with the Enterprise Canvas*

(Tetradian Books, 2010); also summary at
tetradianbooks.com/ecanvas-summary/

- eTOM / Frameworx: see Wikipedia,
en.wikipedia.org/wiki/Enhanced_Telecom_Operations_Map and
en.wikipedia.org/wiki/Frameworx

- FEAF ([US] Federal Enterprise Architecture Framework): see
Wikipedia, en.wikipedia.org/wiki/Federal_Enterprise_Architecture

- Five Elements (*wu xing*): see Wikipedia,
en.wikipedia.org/wiki/Wu_xing

- Hero's Journey story-structure: see
www.thewritersjourney.com/hero's_journey.htm

- Film *Kate & Leopold*: initial version of screenplay,
www.weeklyscript.com/Kate%20And%20Leopold.txt; summary of final-
version plot on Wikipedia, en.wikipedia.org/wiki/Kate_%26_Leopold

- Len Fehskens at The Open Group: see
www.opengroup.org/contacts/bios/fehskens_bio.htm

- 'Manifesto' on power and responsibility in the workplace
[PDF]: tetradianbooks.com/ebook/hss-manifesto.pdf

- Andrew McAfee and 'It's not not about the technology': see
andrewmcafee.org/2007/its_not_not_about_the_technology

- Memory-theatre and 'the art of memory': see Wikipedia,
en.wikipedia.org/wiki/Art_of_memory; also Frances Yates, *The Art of
Memory* (Routledge & Kegan Paul, 1966)

- Narrative-paradigm (Walter Fisher): see Wikipedia,
en.wikipedia.org/wiki/narrative_paradigm

- PDCA (plan, do, check, act): see Wikipedia,
en.wikipedia.org/wiki/PDCA

- John Hagel III, John Seely Brown and Lang Davison, *The
Power of Pull: How Small Moves, Smartly Made, Can Set Big
Things in Motion* (Basic Books, 2010)

- Chris Potts, *recrEAtion: realizing the extraordinary contribution of
your enterprise-architects* (Technics, 2010)

- SCOR (Supply-Chain Operations Reference) framework: see
Wikipedia, en.wikipedia.org/wiki/SCOR

- Gerald M Weinberg, *The Secrets of Consulting: a guide to giving
and getting advice successfully* (Dorset House, 1986) and *More
Secrets of Consulting: the consultant's toolkit* (Dorset House,
2002); see also www.geraldmweinberg.com

- Story-listening: see Anecdote white-paper, *Making the most of
story*, www.anecdote.com.au/whitepapers.php?wpid=27

- Strategy-story and business use of story: see Anecdote, wwww.anecdote.com
- Lao Tsu (tr. Gia Fu Feng and Jane English), *Tao Te Ching* (Wildwood House, 1973)
- The 'This'-game (requirements-elicitation): see weblog.tetradian.com/this-exploratory-game-for-service-oriented-ea/ and weblog.tetradian.com/more-on-the-this-game-for-ea/
- TOGAF (The Open Group Architecture Framework): www.opengroup.org/togaf
- TRAK (architecture framework for London Underground and [UK] Department of Transport): see Wikipedia, en.wikipedia.org/wiki/TRAK
- Transmedia and transmedia-storytelling: see Wikipedia, en.wikipedia.org/wiki/Transmedia_storytelling
- Tuckman Group Dynamics: see Wikipedia, en.wikipedia.org/wiki/Forming-storming-norming-performing
- UML (Unified Modeling Language): see Wikipedia, en.wikipedia.org/wiki/Unified_Modeling_Language
- United Breaks Guitars: see Wikipedia, en.wikipedia.org/wiki/United_Breaks_Guitars
- VPEC-T: see Wikipedia, en.wikipedia.org/wiki/VPEC-T; also Nigel Green and Carl Bate, *Lost in Translation: a handbook for information-systems in the 21st century* (Evolved Technologist Press, 2007)
- Walmart and sustainability: see walmartstores.com/sustainability
- Wicked-problem: see en.wikipedia.org/wiki/Wicked_problem
- Zachman Framework: see www.zifa.com/framework.html or Wikipedia, en.wikipedia.org/wiki/Zachman_Framework

The Tetradian Enterprise Architecture series

The Tetradian Enterprise Architecture series of books present new developments on theory, principles and practice of enterprise-architecture – moving beyond IT to the whole enterprise.

- Tom Graves, *Real Enterprise-Architecture: beyond IT to the whole enterprise* (Tetradian Books, 2008)
- Tom Graves, *Bridging the Silos: enterprise-architecture for IT-architects* (Tetradian Books, 2008)
- Tom Graves: *SEMPER & SCORE: enhancing enterprise effectiveness* (Tetradian Books, 2008)

- Tom Graves, *Power and Response-ability: the human side of systems* (Tetradian Books, 2008)
- Tom Graves, *The Service-Oriented Enterprise: enterprise architecture and viable services* (Tetradian Books, 2009)
- Tom Graves, *Doing Enterprise Architecture: process and practice in the real enterprise* (Tetradian Books, 2009)
- Tom Graves, *Everyday Enterprise Architecture: sensemaking, strategy, structures and solutions* (Tetradian Books, 2010)
- Tom Graves, *Mapping the Enterprise: modelling the enterprise as services with the Enterprise Canvas* (Tetradian Books, 2010)

Other resources

The following are some other links and references that you may find useful in terms of enterprise-as-story:

- Barely Repeatable Processes: see www.thingamy.com
- BMM (Business Motivation Model): see businessrulesgroup.org/bmm.shtml
- Causal Layered Analysis: see Wikipedia, en.wikipedia.org/wiki/Causal_layered_analysis
- Living organisation: see Arie de Geus, *The Living Company: Habits for Survival in a Turbulent Business Environment* (HBR Press, 2002)
- OODA (observe, orient, decide, act): see Wikipedia, en.wikipedia.org/wiki/OODA_loop
- Porter Value-Chain: see Wikipedia, en.wikipedia.org/wiki/Value_chain
- RACI (responsible, assists, consulted, informed): see Wikipedia, en.wikipedia.org/wiki/Responsibility_assignment_matrix
- Shell General Business Principles: www.shell.com/sgbp
- Value-stream mapping: see Wikipedia, en.wikipedia.org/wiki/Value_stream_mapping
- VRMG (vision, role, mission, goal): see www.slideshare.net/tetradian/vision-role-mission-goal-a-framework-for-business-motivation

www.ingramcontent.com/pod-product-compliance
Lightning Source LLC
Chambersburg PA
CBHW021603210326
41599CB00010B/571